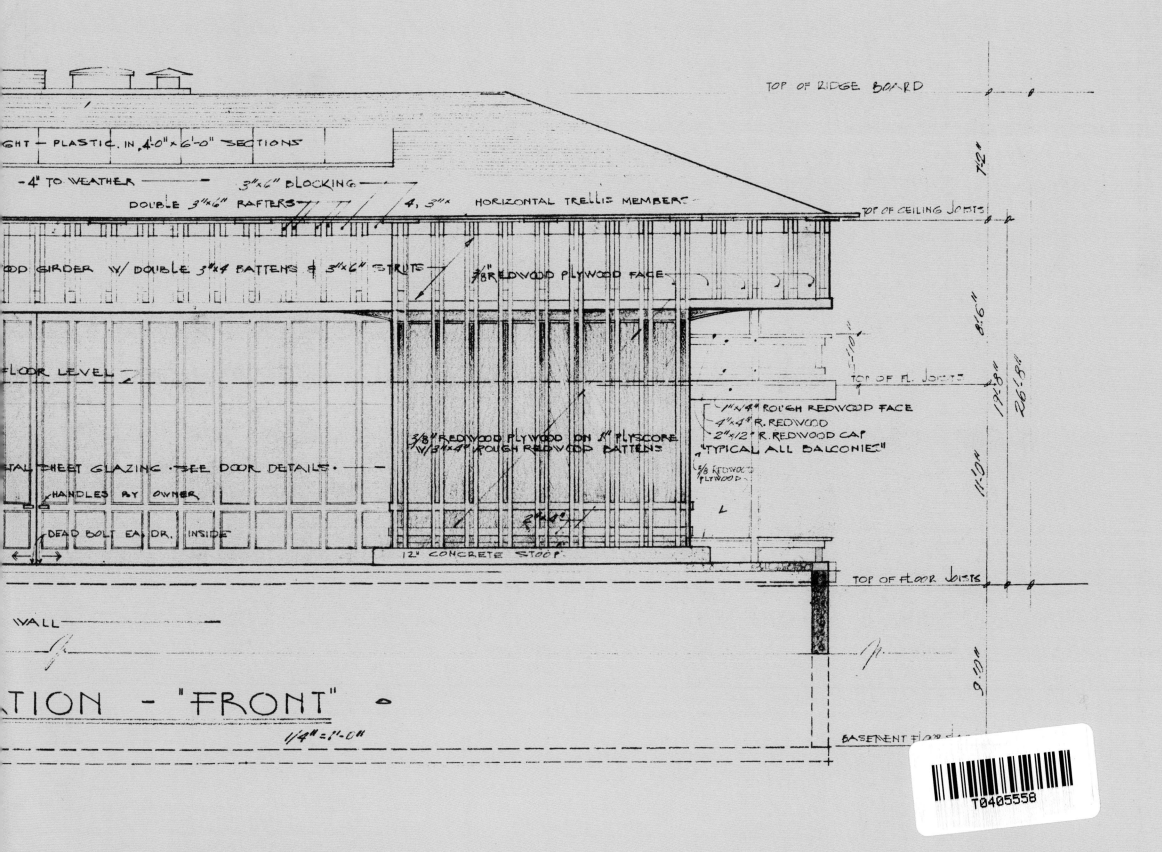

GHT - PLASTIC IN 4'-0" × 6'-0" SECTIONS

-4" TO WEATHER — 3"×6" BLOCKING

DOUBLE 3"×6" RAFTERS — 4, 3"× HORIZONTAL TRELLIS MEMBERS

OD GIRDER W/ DOUBLE 3"×4 BATTENS & 3"×6" STRUTS — 3/8" REDWOOD PLYWOOD FACE

FLOOR LEVEL 2

3/8" REDWOOD PLYWOOD ON 5" PLYSCORE W/ 3"×4" ROUGH REDWOOD BATTENS

TAL SHEET GLAZING · SEE DOOR DETAILS ·

HANDLES BY OWNER

DEAD BOLT EA DR. INSIDE

12" CONCRETE STOOP

1"×4" ROUGH REDWOOD FACE
4"×4" R. REDWOOD
2"×12" R. REDWOOD CAP
"TYPICAL ALL BALCONIES"

3/8 REDWOOD PLYWOOD

TOP OF RIDGE BOARD

TOP OF CEILING JOISTS

TOP OF FL. JOISTS

TOP OF FLOOR JOISTS

BASEMENT FLOOR

7'-2"
8'-6"
12'-8"
26'-8"
11'-9"
9'-10"

WALL

TION - "FRONT" ·

1/4" = 1'-0"

DESIGN LEGACY OF

John Marsh Davis

EARLY CAREER: WOOD EXPRESSIONISM 1961–1979

HANS R. BALDAUF

Above Early Scheme of Nash Residence.

DESIGN LEGACY OF

John Marsh Davis

EARLY CAREER: WOOD EXPRESSIONISM 1961–1979

Introduction & Project Essays by HANS R. BALDAUF
With a Biographical Essay by DAVID SHEFF
Principal Photography by BRUCE DAMONTE AND R. BRAD KNIPSTEIN

HANS R. BALDAUF

OSCAR RIERA OJEDA
PUBLISHERS

The publication of Design Legacy of John Marsh Davis, Early Career: Wood Expressionism 1961-1979 is made possible by Katy Davis Song and Richard W Moore III.

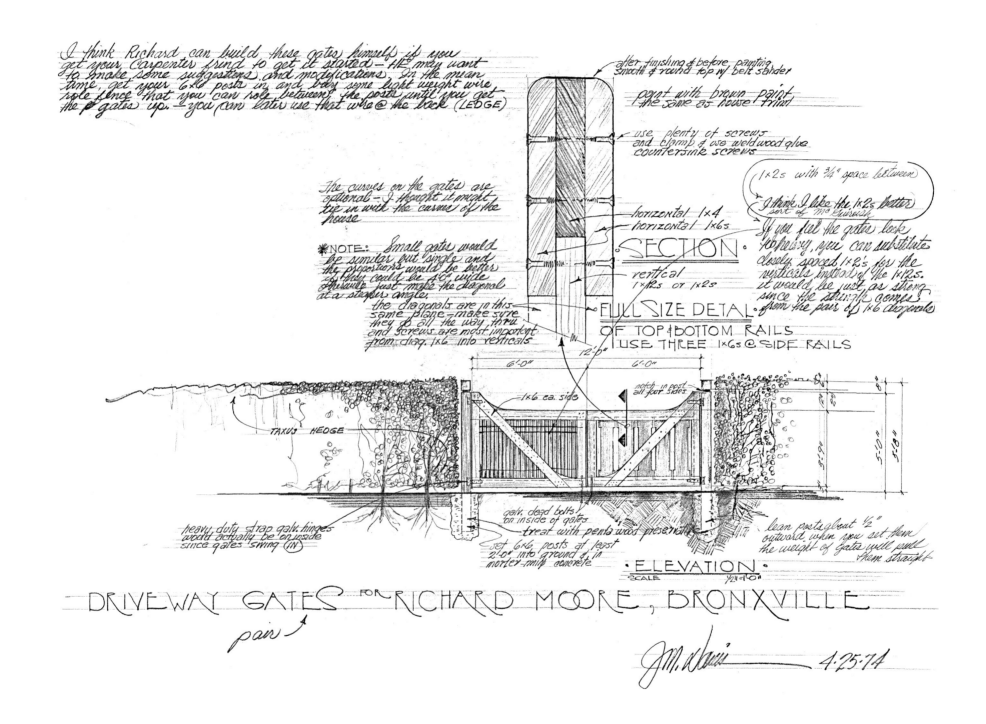

Above Drawing of Moore house driveway gates. 1974.

TABLE OF CONTENTS

ACKNOWLEDGEMENTS

In 2012, our firm was hired to renovate the original Joseph Phelps Vineyards winery building into a visitor's center with additional offices. I had known the building for years, but had not known anything about its architect, John Marsh Davis, beyond the fact that he had also designed the Souverain Winery (now Rutherford Hill), and a house out at Stinson Beach.

Finding little published on Davis, who had passed away three years prior, Bill Phelps directed me to Katy Davis Song, Davis' niece who had archived his life's work. Katy kindly gave us access to this and Davis' photo albums – and the adventure of putting this book together began.

As an architect, I am interested in presenting a body of work which I find inspiring. I hope that others will find it so as well, and more importantly, preserve these amazing structures as they age and pass into new hands.

I have been aided by many individuals who have recounted memories of John and his work. Among these is Ann Dickerson Lind who informed me that years before I actually met John at a dinner at her home in Sausalito. I think we discussed landscape and not architecture and as I was unaware of who he was, I fear I missed an amazing opportunity to talk with a master. In many ways, the research on this book is my effort to make up for that missed opportunity.

I want to thank Myralin Whitaker, Lisa Whitaker, and Gina Field for their help. I had a long conversation with Joe Phelps about, his collaborations with John over the years which was very valuable. Donald MacDonald, who had both gone to the Architecture School at the University of Oklahoma and had worked with John, provided many insights that helped me begin to understand John's education and the group of graduates who came to California. James Lino shared his and his father's experiences building for John. Bill Phelps and Ross Sullivan both shared stories of the joy of being laborers on winery projects that their families built. The impact of Davis' projects on the client's children is chronicled in David Sheff's essay but was also brought up to me by David Thacher, who, with his siblings, spent a year living next to the construction site of their parent's house. Cynthia Wayburn shared the joys her husband had working with Davis to create his house in Medina, Washington.

In the fall of 2021, I was honored to accompany Katy Davis Song to the University of Oklahoma Architecture School where she donated Davis' drawings to the to the archive that the University of Oklahoma has created of graduates who helped create the American School. This archive has been built through the vision of Dean Hans Butzer and Director of the Division of Architecture Stephanie Pilat. Their work has been instrumental in helping me put Davis in context with the other students of Bruce Goff.

I am very grateful to David Sheff and his essay on John and the Barbour family that he married into for all their wonderful stories about John Marsh Davis. Nancy Barbour is perhaps Davis' greatest champion. They are clients who were also collaborators.

It is our hope that this will be one of the first of many monographs that celebrate the architects of the American School whose work is archived at the University. (Mickey Muennig's monograph was written prior to the donation of his archive and is an excellent book.)

This book has had a ten-year gestation and many hands at our office have touched it and I thank them all. Special mention needs to go to Julia Stenderup, Peter Sterling, Esther Sam, Robert Holloway, Hana Davis and my business partner Chris von Eckartsberg.

The book is for the passionate guardians of John's work, both his original clients and those who have been fortunate to become guardians since their creation.

The book is dedicated to my wife, Marian and our wonderful children, Fritz and Liesl who have put up with my architectural detours.

—

Previous spread Entryway trellis to Joseph Phelps Vineyards. **Opposite page** Joseph Phelps Vineyards visitor center, redesigned by BCV Architecture + Interiors. San Francisco, June 2022.

INTRODUCTION

John Marsh Davis Jr. was born in the heartland of Oklahoma on October 12, 1931. He received a Bachelor of Arts from the University of Oklahoma at Norman, graduating in 1955. At the time, the architecture department was led by Bruce Goff – perhaps Frank Lloyd Wright's most inventive follower. As a student of Goff's at the University of Oklahoma, Davis can be properly thought of as a member of the American School. After serving four years in the U.S. Navy, which included a tour of Japan, Davis worked as an apprentice at the architecture firm of Reynolds and Morrison in Oklahoma City.

In 1961, Davis moved to Sausalito and began a long career in which he became well known for his handcrafted homes in Marin and Sonoma Counties, along with wineries in Napa. Each of his projects exhibited an originality and wit that he became known for, working closely with clients and creating friendships that lasted throughout his lifetime.

Davis established his practice in the San Francisco Bay Area with the design and construction of his home and studio in Sausalito – beginning the approximately two decades of work covered in this book, a period I have labeled "Wood Expressionism." While his work from the early 1980s through the mid-1990s expanded on many of the same themes as the early work, the projects became increasingly refined and layered, and deserves to be explored more in a subsequent study.

In his later years, Davis evolved his focus towards his love for nature, and designed gardens and landscapes. Davis passed away on February 22, 2009 but his legacy lives on through wineries across Napa and Sonoma – Joseph Phelps Vineyards, Souverain Winery, Chateau Souverain, and Sullivan Vineyards – along with numerous homes throughout Northern California and beyond.

Opposite page John Marsh Davis on construction site.

A MIDWESTERN RENEGADE COMES TO NORTHERN CALIFORNIA

by David Sheff

"Make no little plans," the architect Daniel Burnham said. "They have no magic to stir men's blood and probably will not themselves be realized." In colored pencil, John Marsh Davis, Jr. drew those words in architectural block letters on paper that he framed and displayed in his homes and on jobsites – and he followed Burnham's advice. John made no little plans. His creations – homes, offices, wineries and gardens – stirred the blood; they still stir mine.

John once told me he didn't know there was a job called "architect" when he was a child. "I didn't know the power of architecture," he said, "how it can elevate life." Once John said, "A good building feeds the mind and imagination as much as a great book or painting or opera."

Born on October 12, 1931, John grew up on the Oklahoma prairie in the town of Altus, which is located thirty miles from the Oklahoma-Texas border in the southwest corner of the state at the intersection of what are now U.S. Highways 62 and 283. Altus began as a settlement on Bitter Creek, where there was a trading post on the Great Western Cattle Trail. Then called Frazer, cowboys driving herds north-ward often stopped to buy buttermilk at the depot; the town became known as Buttermilk Station. A flash flood nearly destroyed Frazer in 1891, and the residents moved the town to higher ground two-and-a-half miles to the east. They renamed it Altus to celebrate its relatively high (1400 feet) elevation. In the early 1900s, the town was a thriving agricultural trade and distribution center. Wheat, cotton, and grain sorghum were grown on farms on the periphery of town.

When John was a young boy, there was an oil strike on the land of a family that lived in town. "It was like the *Beverly Hillbillies* TV show," John said. Like the Clampetts on television, the family moved from Oklahoma to Beverly Hills, where they bought a lot and hired "the most expensive architect they could find," instructing him to design them a grand mansion. The family moved into the lavish home and invited their neighbors to a party. No one came. "They were snubbed," John said. "All the money in the world couldn't erase the fact that they were Okies." And so they retreated to Altus, where they used the same architectural plans to build an exact replica of the house they'd constructed in Beverly Hills.

John said, in retrospect, the house was a garish monstrosity, out of place in Altus, but, in its immensity and impact on the town, at the time he thought it was fantastic. John told me about visiting the construction site. First he noticed the quiet and a mounting sense of something coming. Then it did come: graders and loaders and cement mixers and trucks leaving stacks of rebar and framing wood. For a while, it seemed as if all anyone in Altus talked about was the building rising from the Oklahoma dirt. As it grew, John snuck onto the jobsite and peeked at the cryptic plans. "It was a glimpse of another language and a different world – a picture of everything changing." As the house grew, John said he witnessed "the power of a building to excite."

Opposite page Drawing by Davis celebrating a quote by Daniel Burnham, 1969.

"MAKE NO LITTLE PLANS,
THEY HAVE NO MAGIC TO STIR MEN'S BLOOD AND
PROBABLY THEMSELVES WILL NOT BE REALIZED.
MAKE BIG PLANS; AIM HIGH IN HOPE AND WORK,
REMEMBERING THAT A NOBLE, LOGICAL DIAGRAM
ONCE RECORDED WILL NEVER DIE, BUT LONG
AFTER WE ARE GONE WILL BE A LIVING THING,
ASSERTING ITSELF WITH EVER-GROWING INSISTENCY.
REMEMBER THAT OUR SONS AND GRANDSONS ARE GOING
TO DO THINGS THAT WOULD STAGGER US. LET YOUR
WATCH WORD BE ORDER AND YOUR BEACON BEAUTY."

D. H. BURNHAM

1967

J·M·D
96 Santa Rosa Ave.
Sausalito, CA 94965

Above left First Street of Altus, Oklahoma – 1910s. **Above right** Cotton Yard in Altus, Oklahoma – early 1900s. **Below left** Davis in US Navy uniform. **Below middle** Davis (on the right) with his sister Barbara Davis Moore and her husband, Richard W. Moore Jr. at the Harrison residence in 1962/63. **Below right** Davis' 50th Birthday with the Barbour family, 12 October 1981.

John's father and uncle owned twenty cotton gins, but his asthma prevented him from going into the family business. He felt alienated from other boys, whose lives revolved around sports and working outdoors. When he was a teenager, he took a bike trip to Europe. "That's where his education in arts and architecture really began," according to Katy Song, John's niece.

Back home in Altus, John determined to become an architect and enrolled, in 1951, in the renowned University of Oklahoma School of Architecture, where he was a student of the legendary Bruce Goff.

After graduating, he enlisted in the Navy and became a commissioned officer serving on the USS *Philippine Sea*. Throughout his later life, he would often reflect on the influence of his time in in the service in Europe and Asia, where he absorbed the architecture and design of buildings and gardens. Back home in Altus, he worked for a local architect before moving to the Bay Area in 1961, settling in Marin County, where he built a home for himself in Sausalito, then an artist enclave. The home was modest in terms of square footage, but it was thrilling to behold. It was the first glimpse of a vision that would get stronger and more confident over time.

My mother-in-law, Nancy Barbour, saw John's home when it was featured on the cover of *California Home Magazine*. Nancy and her husband, Donald, a physician, were looking for an architect to design a home on a two-acre parcel of woodsy land on the hills above Kentfield, a half hour north of the Golden Gate Bridge. She loved the Davis home – the way the building was part of nature and invited it inside, the outlandish scale – and called John.

The home he designed for the Barbours is a testament to no small plans. It's essentially a redwood board-and-batten rectangle crowned with extravagant trellises upon which hang wisteria, but massive, with twenty-foot-high floor-to-ceiling windows. Inside, the rectangle is divided by sliding doors, which function like shoji screens to separate the "library" and kitchen from the great room. It has rough wood floors on which the kids would get splinters. A generation later, visiting grandchildren swung on a rope swing, which still hangs from the rough redwood beams in the center of the great room. (These kids grew up thinking it was normal to have a swing set inside a house.) Even with a fireplace as big as one in a castle, it was almost always icy cold in the winter because there was no insulation (construction was completed in 1965).

One entire wall opens to the outside with an enormous sliding glass-and-wood door. As it was described by a critic in *Bay Area Style*, the effect is thrilling. "The long side of this house simply rolls away," wrote architect David Weingarten. "What was inside is, now, outside; what was a house is, now, a porch. What's more, the house now appears structurally unsupported, held aloft by unseen forces. (The secret is an ingenious truss.)" i

The large doors open to a garden created by John with the renowned landscape architect Thomas Church. The highly sought-after Church agreed to design the garden only because (he admitted) he liked the sound of Nancy's "husky" voice on the phone (she had a cold when she called to ask). He charged $100 and a bottle of vodka. "Young man, get your pencil out," Church said to John. "I have a horrible headache, and I'll only be here three hours." They created a small, terraced garden with twisting Japanese maples in huge planter boxes. When the big doors are closed, it's like a framed postcard from Kyoto. When they're open, it's an extension of the great room, where Nancy, Don and John sat in boxy McGuire chairs sipping bourbon and water on warm fall evenings.

Weingarten called the house John built for Nancy and Don, "Goffian in its flamboyant extravagance" and, a half century later, it still takes the breath away of anyone who stops by. Nancy said that living in a John Marsh Davis home influenced every aspect of her life. "John taught me how to see beauty in details," she says. "As I grew up, I noticed every corner, the trim, the way the boards intersected... John anticipated every sightline, the way the light would filter in at different times of year. Everything is lined up. Everywhere you look, there's something dramatic and spectacular."

My wife Karen, an artist, was inspired by the house and by John himself. Karen and her sister and brother, Susan and Steven, thought of John as a kind of James Bond character or rock star who showed up in a Bentley with an enormous Saint Bernard or, later, a pair of unruly golden retrievers bounding out of the car when he arrived. His relationship with the family didn't end when the house was complete; he became a lifelong friend. He never stopped redesigning the interior of the Barbour home. He would show up with antique Hargrave lamps, Persian rugs and random objects from shopping sprees abroad or at flea markets.

Over the years, John designed a half dozen homes for himself. Each was uniquely spectacular. Karen remembers the feeling of walking into them. John prepared for the arrival of guests as if it was the opening of a theater production. He watered the gravel paths because he liked the deeper and richer gray the water created. No matter the weather, a fire raged in the fireplace. (John burned whatever was handy, including old chairs and tabletops and, once, his friend Charlie Merrill's sails.) He blasted opera music from built-in stereo systems; it was almost as if he'd choreographed the entrance to the garden to the opening of *Don Giovanni*. You reached the front door and entered the house at a crescendo in the overture. Dinner would be roasted leg of lamb with fresh mint, roasted potatoes with parsley, a salad of lettuces from the garden and store-bought cookies for dessert.

The houses were perpetually morphing. There would always be something exciting to see, including drawings (John's own highly realistic figurative drawings were exquisite) and paintings on the walls. A straight-backed Ralph Lauren couch would appear by the fireplace, facing a patio with a trestle table he designed and built out of redwood leftover from the construction of the house. In the corner of the great room, John had placed a pair of Sir Edwin Lutyens Napoleon chairs that had arrived by ship from London. Not only did the furniture change, entire rooms would appear and disappear or reconfigure when, seemingly overnight, John would add walls or partial walls or remove them completely.

Both in his own houses and gardens and those John designed for others, he used mirrors to work magic, creating optical illusions of perspective, dimension and area. Inside, he used mirrors to extend bookshelves (built-in bookshelves were ubiquitous in John's houses; his were lined with books and magazines about art and architecture in addition to meticulously curated oversized photo albums, which were artworks in themselves) and windows, to multiply beams, mullions and moldings. Mirrors brought the outside – the gardens or the San Francisco Bay itself – inside, erasing exterior walls. Outside, he used mirrors to extend paths, hedges and views. "The trick is to use mirrors where they'll let you see architectural details but not your own reflection," he said. Because of the mirrors, out-of-scale structures and other architectural sleight-of-hand, an 1800 sq foot home would feel like a mansion, a small section of a garden would feel like Versailles and another would be like the garden at a Buddhist monastery in Nara.

Above John Marsh Davis perspective drawing of Barbour Residence design, showing entry bridge with scheme featuring pool but replaced by a garden designed by Thomas Church in the final scheme.

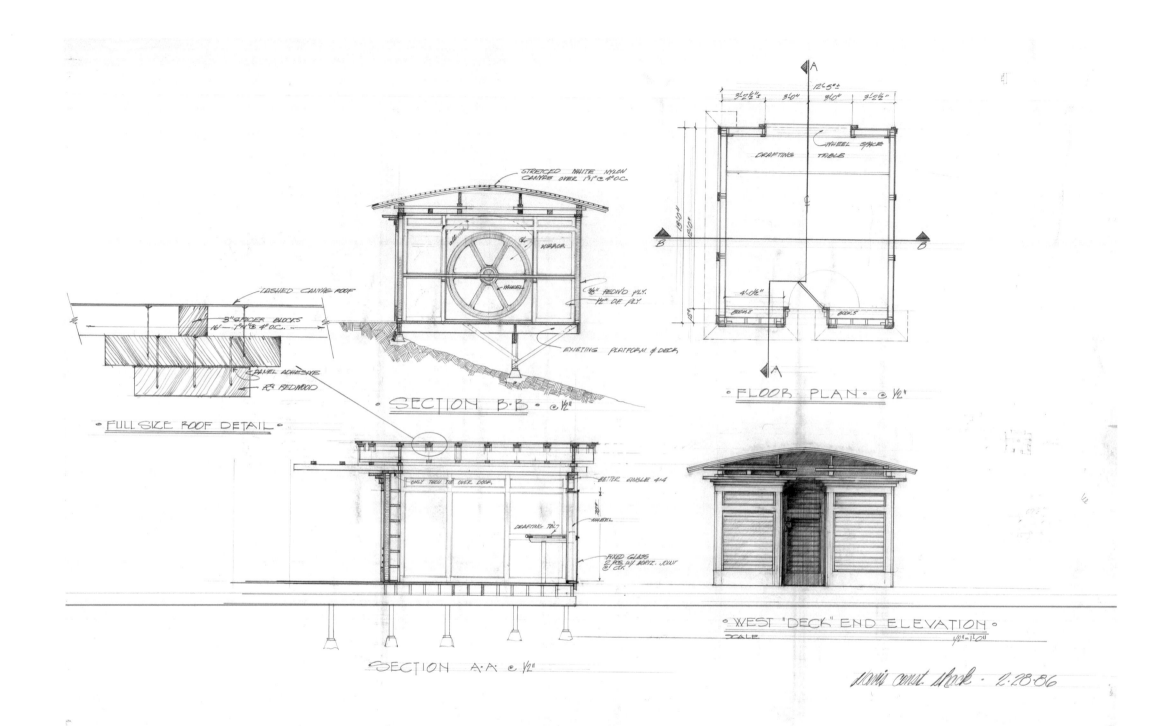

Above Drawing of Davis construction shack on Inverness, CA property. 1986. **Opposite page** View of great room from garden and view of garden from the great room.

Indeed, gardens held a special place in John's imagination. In many of his later commissions, he would insist on designing the gardens himself as he came to believe that setting was the most important element in a great building. "The house should serve the garden, not the other way around," he said. Indeed, John's gardens were as dynamic and dramatic as the houses were. Sections of garden – circles of lavender or a wall of white roses – would disappear one week and, the next, be replaced by bamboo columns, which John meticulously sculpted. Depending on where you stood, you would be confronted with different but always dramatic vistas. John built structures – trellises, a dove cote, a garden pagoda – to create focal points and delineate outdoor "rooms" as well as to hide things that he thought were ugly (water meters, a propane tank) – and also to hide illegal structures from the planning commissioner.

In the late 1990s, John was working on an acre parcel of land he'd bought in Inverness, a northern California town on the Tomales Bay, where he experimented for five years with a garden that combined elements of those he'd seen in Europe (lines of Italian cypress, endless boxwood and pitasporin hedges and rows of hydrangea in huge terra cotta pots) and Japan (mazes of black bamboo and winding, stone-and-moss paths). He constructed a single-room cabin with one entire wall built around the positive mold for a gear from the San Francisco cable car system with an outdoor kitchen and shower, all hidden behind walls of hedges and a disappearing gate. He experimented with hedges, trees, flower beds and terraced lawns. As critic Fred A. Bernstein wrote in *Metropolitan Home*, "Davis spent years creating the lawns, hedges and decks that he refers to as 'the structure of the garden.' Then, with those structural elements as a frame, he began painting the hillside with flowers – luminaria, lilac, agapanthus – distributed so that, as a good fireworks display, there's always an explosion of color somewhere." [ii]

He'd get to the house at some point. "A house can go up overnight," he said, "but a great garden takes years to evolve."

When John decided to move to the San Juan Islands because the Bay Area was getting too crowded, Karen bought the garden. (John returned to Sausalito after a couple years; he missed his friends.) John revised (expanded) plans he'd drawn for himself for a home. He worked with James Lino, a master contractor whose father had also worked with John, to create a house that Bernstein described "as perfectly crafted as a Chinese puzzle and nearly as intriguing." It was described elsewhere as "as intricate and beautiful as a jewel box" and "as finely made – and as handsome – as a Japanese tansu."

As always in John's designs, the scale is jolting. Each room has a steeply pitched roof covered in copper-clad tiles from Italy. Bernstein wrote, "(the house) resembles a series of garden pavilions rather than single massive structure. Inside, however, the pavilions soar."

In the book *American Style*, critic Dylan Landis described the scale: "The mantle over the Rumford fireplace... stands higher than 8 feet. French doors and windows are 10 feet tall, and the timber-and-glass ceiling soars to 22 feet.... Redwood, a staple of contemporary California houses, is treated with the fine, almost intricate workman-

Opposite page Former construction shack, now garden cabin of Barbour-Sheff Residence. **This page** Barbour-Sheff Residence. Inverness, CA.

Opposite page View in the main garden up towards the art studio of the Barbour-Sheff Residence **Above** Elevation of the Barbour-Sheff fireplace by John Marsh Davis.

ship of the Arts and Crafts period, and the serenity of the space is clearly borrowed from the Japanese." iii Karen and John mixed together the Giverny green interior paint with subtle differences in hue from one wall to the next. Outside, the trim is painted what we came to call John Davis Blue: a smokey, greyish blue that's a combination of Rust-Oleum marine-grade royal blue, flat black and white. The color is ubiquitous on window and door trim, outdoor furniture and architectural elements hidden throughout the garden. Versions of it are seen in most of the homes and wineries John designed.

Architectural plans for John served as guidelines, but nothing was sacrosanct. He improvised, frequently ignoring the drawn and engineered (and approved by the county) plans when he got a new idea. Using a grease pencil on a piece of plywood, he would sketch designs that came to him the night before. It wasn't inexpensive working with John because he experimented until he came up with what he wanted and meanwhile the client paid the bills. John designed and Jim built beautiful shelves that crossed the windows in the Inverness kitchen, allowing views of the gardens in the front and back of the house. When they were finished, John stared at them for a while and then judged them "too Hansel and Gretley." He instructed Jim to rip them out and start again, this time drawing (on the floor) a simpler, more classical design. Beauty for John wasn't about perfection; he wanted and created flaws. In one home he designed, he rolled boulders and bowling balls on a just-laid, sanded and varnished wood floor that he thought was too shiny and perfect. (The owner trusted John but nonetheless held back tears.) Another time, John bought two beautiful Persian rugs but didn't like their "newness." With the help of Karen's brother, Steven, he nailed them to the roof of his house so the weather would make them "come alive."

Designing our house as it went up, John would stare into what was then empty space, describing the way he wanted a skylight built that would allow in direct sunlight in winter and diffused light in summer, all softened and framed (dramatically) by a latticework of slats of redwood. John spent days working with Jim to get huge interior mirrors aligned exactly right so that you could see endless vistas of the garden and the redwood fireplace mantle from a million angles depending on where you stand. In certain light, you can forget you're indoors, because the garden floods in through the giant French doors and windows and reflects infinitely in the floor-to-ceiling mirrors. Once someone asked incredulously, "How many dogs do you have?" We had two, but because of those mirrors, it appeared as if we had a pack.

Over the years, John built perhaps a hundred private residences, each unique and uniquely remarkable, and he designed magnificent commercial buildings, including wineries in the Napa Valley – for Chateau Souverain, Joseph Phelps Winery, and Souverain Winery. Nature is at the core of all of his structures. Like those in his own houses, signature John Marsh elements include interior rooms that flow seamlessly into exterior garden rooms and unorthodox building placement that takes advantage of whatever is unique about the site. (Our garden seems infinitely larger because he placed the home at the edge instead of the middle of the property.)

John worked with master craftspeople, and he was an excellent carpenter in his own right. Steven, a close friend of John's, worked with him on some of John's personal projects. They were sitting in the living room of John's Sausalito home when, one night, he seemed distracted, staring at the ceiling. Suddenly he told Steve to grab the tools; he'd decided the house needed a skylight. Though it was the middle of the night, he and Steve climbed on the roof, cut out a huge square and built a grid of boards to filter the light. (They added glass the next day.) Rather than replacing a cracked built-in mirror that covered a wall that reflected the glittering-blue San Francisco Bay upon which sailboats floated like Lotus pedals, John covered the crack with iron shapes that evoke Frank Lloyd Wright's stained glass windows. Once John hand-painted a Persian rug on the floor in front of the fireplace as an experiment in trompe l'oeil. It was meticulously rendered and exquisite, and then one day it was gone.

Steve remembers being with John when he was considering a parcel of land or a house. John would stand completely still and just stare in quiet, impenetrable contemplation. "I always wanted to be a part of that contemplation." I know that feeling and the look John would get when he was inspired. It's impossible to describe watching from the outside an artist's mind creating, but it was thrilling. When John came out of a trance, he'd grab whatever was nearby he could draw on.

In an article about John's Sausalito home on Santa Rosa Street – a masterpiece in which he spent the final twenty years of his life – in the *Wall Street Journal*, critic Nancy Keates notes that John "cherished confrontation and agitation." [iv]

Above John Marsh Davis on the construction site of the Barbour-Sheff residence.

I grew up in a tract home where the houses were identical other than the choice of color of bricks and landscaping (a lawn or red-rock garden). I didn't know how a building could change and define a life – how wood and nails and glass and mirrors can inspire – until I watched John work, got to know him and lived in a product of his imagination. After living in a John Davis designed home for more than 30 years, I still look around the house and garden and see John here – his beloved dogs at his side, panting, wreaking havoc – though he passed away in 2009, I really do still see him here – in the macro and micro of the house and garden – the grand vision and a million intimate details, forever challenging me – confronting and agitating me and us all and inspiring us to make no little plans.

Sources
Weingarten, David. Bay Area Style. Rizzoli International Publications, 2004, p 127.
Bernstein, Fred A. "The House That Grew Up in a Garden." Metropolitan Home, Nov. 1994, p. 100.
Landis, Dylan. Metropolitan Home: American Style. Clarkson Potter Publishers, 1999, p 38.
Keates, Nancy. "Smooth Jazz Meets Stormy Design." Wall Street Journal, Sept. 19, 2004.

THE AMERICAN SCHOOL MEETS THE BAY TRADITION

by Hans Baldauf

John Marsh Davis produced an extraordinary body of built work that included primarily private homes and wineries, as well as a variety of other building types. The work is a highly personal synthesis of powerful influences. His designs show the influence of his education at the University of Oklahoma under the direction of Bruce Goff and of the San Francisco Bay tradition, which he absorbed upon moving to northern California in 1961.Goff was the foremost educator to champion the legacy of Louis Sullivan and Frank Lloyd Wright. The Bay Area tradition dates from the 1880s and is exemplified in the work of Bernard Maybeck and Willis Polk. A second and a third generation of the Bay tradition is also commonly refered to. Among the members of these latter generations was Warren Callister whose work was an inspiration to Davis.

Callister – like Davis – was inspired by Maybeck and the first Bay tradition. Both Callister and Davis spent time in Japan (Davis while in the Navy) and the traditions of Japanese woodwork are a hallmark of their work. At the University of Oklahoma, students were encouraged to explore non-Western architectural traditions, so it is not surprising that Davis would find these influences a source of inspiration when he came to live and build in Northern California.

Davis' work throughout his career was profoundly shaped by his education under Bruce Goff. Goff was the head of the Architecture department at the University of Oklahoma from 1943 to 1955. John Marsh Davis graduated from the school in Goff's final year, so he had the benefit of studying under Goff's evolved pedagogical model for the full time he was at the University.

Above From Left To Right: Louis Sullivan, Frank Lloyd Wright, Bruce Goff and Bernard Maybeck.

Above Beer Garden – Student Project under Bruce Goff, University of Oklahoma Architecture School.

Goff's approach was to push students to understand and express their own ideas. The result of this was a group of renegade designers whose work is defined by the singular pursuit of their ideas. This has come to be called the American School, a term first coined by Donald MacDonald who also attended the University of Oklahoma.

In his essay, "Pragmatic Thinking in the Continuous Present," part of the compilation *Renegades: Bruce Goff and the American School of Architecture*, Christopher Curtis Mead writes:

"The American School of architecture is known for its stubbornly individual, wildly unconventional, and structurally exuberant buildings. Grounded in the path-breaking precedents of Louis Sullivan and Frank Lloyd Wright, this school extends from the open-ended teaching of Bruce Goff, ... [whose students] were encouraged by Goff's example to find their own way to create works that defy categorization except for a shared insistence on standing outside the mainstream. Less a style than an attitude, the American School questions the very norms of architecture and culture" (Guido et al. 15).

According to Mead, Goff absorbed Sullivan's thinking that "every problem contains and suggests its own solution," (Sullivan, 164) but he took it further by realizing that every problem could lead to multiple solutions. Goff absorbed the idea of the "continuous present" as articulated by Gertrude Stein, which led to three interlocking principles of design:

"1. Design is an open-ended process that grows organically from the architect's experience and can potentially produce multiple solutions;
2. Any work of architecture should be a multivalent spatial continuum that can be entered at multiple points and taken in multiple directions, moving beyond the classical sequence of front, center, and back along a controlling axis;
3. Every work of architecture finally escapes a fixed meaning (or even multiple fixed meanings) for shifting interpretations shape both by our individual experiences and by our changing perceptions over time." (Guido et al. 22)

Bruce Goff came to teach at the school of architecture at the University of Oklahoma in 1942 and was named Chairman in 1943. He taught at the school through 1955 when he chose to resign because his homosexuality was not supported within the Norman community, although he did have support within the university. Goff and later his students who remained as professors, including Herb Greene, created a dynamic academic community at the University of Oklahoma.

The canon of architectural history taught at OU was diverse, encompassing cultures from around the world and across time. Goff argued that most academic institutions of the time were ignorant of the richness of non-Western architecture from regions such as Egypt, India, China, Japan, Central America and wonderful ethnic constructions by non-architect builders all over the world. Students were taught to appreciate not only nonwestern architecture, but also the art and potential of their own surroundings: Everyday objects, the natural landscape and the design of American Indian tribes (Guido et al. 6).

In the absence of historical models to reappropriate or contemporary masters to imitate, American School architects drew inspiration from a few key things: particular sites, clients, and programs. The local conditions – the

Above Herb Greene and his project, the Joyce House in Snyder, Oklahoma 1961.

Above Road to the Ikuta Shrine, Kobe, Japan ca. 1900. Hand-colored albumen print, Unknown Photographer.

existing landscape, the climate, and local materials – provided a foundation for innovative designs without formal constraints. Individual clients and the programs they desired helped individual designers to create original works for each and every project (Guido et al. 7).

It is clear that Davis was deeply influenced by his education at the University of Oklahoma. Each of his projects is a profound exploration of its site, program and client's desires.

The architect Herb Greene graduated from the architecture school at the University of Oklahoma a couple of years prior to Davis. He would later return to teach at the University prior to moving on to teach at the University of Kentucky where he published *Mind and Image* in 1976. In this "essay" Greene articulates a design philosophy that grew out of Goff's teaching at Oklahoma and his own research into the nature of perception. As Davis did not write much about or lecture on his work, Greene's words help elucidate some of what Davis seems to have explored in his work.

"Another way of looking at the problem of time and timelessness in an image is to consider the more abstract pattern of its design. In a successful work of art, the pattern of the whole conveys a feeling that essential relationships exists between the data in the image and the world beyond the image. The result is a feeling that there is something important to be unraveled in the manner in which the pattern of the image is connected to the world. I first felt the force of this idea while studying the floor plans of Frank Lloyd Wright" (Greene, 51).

"In the Shinto architectural tradition of old Japan, the expression of character through textures is an important concept. This tradition intuitively accepted the intercommunication of the senses which has been ignored by the western tradition…. It follows that the shapes of trees produced by natural forces, the textures and grain patterns of wood and the changes to wood due to weathering are recognized and become the symbolic content of Architecture" (Greene, 69).

Green's concepts of the "pattern of the whole" and the texture of wood are fundamental elements of Davis' wood expressionist period. The pattern of the wood structural systems that underlie all of Davis' designs are a starting point. These systems generally are in service of and celebrate a great sheltering roof that provides the signifying form of the building. The play between structure and roof is often made complex, forcing the observer to try and discern the pattern of the whole. This is nowhere more evident than in the Thacher Residence and the Phoenix Leasing Building. Occasionally, Davis integrated actual mirrors within his projects to further challenge the reality of perception. The reverence for wood grain and texture can be seen throughout his work. Davis' wood trusses can be read as quasi living elements particularly where they become the armature for vines.

Another key features of Davis' work is the merging of landscape and architecture. Davis' projects simultaneously merge with their landscapes and float above the environment. The great entry trellis at the Joseph Phelps Winery connects to the hillside and then jumps over the entry drive to split the building leading the visitor out to the view of the valley beyond. At the Barnett Residence and the Sullivan Winery, the main floor decks float above the vines.

The hearth forms a feature in many of Davis' residential projects – much as they do in Frank Lloyd Wright's houses. These hearths, often exaggerated in scale, provide a counterpoint to the wood structure and the roof – often it seems that the structure is dancing with the solidity of the hearth – or perhaps more appropriately, dancing around the hearth.

Just as Davis' hearths are of exaggerated scale, he often used very tall doors in his projects – these custom-built doors lead outside and provide a vertical contrast to the horizon beyond. The doors at once assert the importance of the human occupant as a standing person and make us realize that we are part of a much larger system.

It is tempting to think of Davis as the solitary artist. There are drawings in his hand that are signed by him noting a time well past midnight. Davis' niece Katy Davis Song says that "renegade" is the perfect way to describe her uncle, because he was not interested in living by the rules. In fact, he never became a licensed architect, but like all architects, he did rely on the work of others. The lower floor of his San Carlos Avenue house was set up as an office and for a while, he maintained an office up in Napa Valley. Central to these efforts, it seems was a set of associations that reached back to the University of Oklahoma. Violeta Autumn, an early female graduate of the school, and Davis maintained a joint practice for a period of time as is indicated by title blocks bearing both of their names in his archive.

Oklahoma graduate Donald MacDonald was a colleague and long-time supporter of Davis and was a part of a group of like-minded architects, some of whom also went to the University with Davis and MacDonald. He helped

Opposite page Calle Del Sierra Residence, Barbour Residence, 174 Harrison Residence. **Above** Nash Residence.

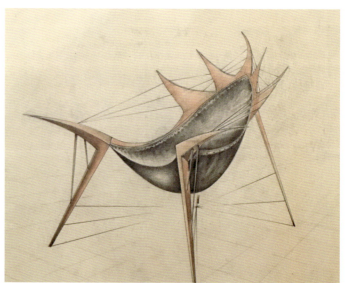

Above Donald MacDonald, East Span of the San Francisco Bay Bridge; Mickey Muennig's studio, 1975 photo, Violeta Autumn, Design for a chair.

get them all published in several numbers of the Japanese periodical *a+u*. These included Oklahoma University graduates Davis, Richard Whitaker and Mickey Muennig. MacDonald created the notion of the "American School" of architects for an exhibition in London to refer to the students of Bruce Goff.

California was fertile ground for the architects of the American School. MacDonald's work explored the urban realm and now the intersection of architecture, engineering and sculpture in bridge design. Davis and Muennig's work confronts the California landscape in all of its drama, Muennig in Big Sur and Davis in Marin, Sonoma and Napa.

In their essay "The Legacy and Lessons of the American School," Hans Butzer, Angela Person and Christian Dagg observe that "By looking at how the American School laid the foundation for a responsive type of practice, we can begin to answer questions of legacy and relevance" (Guido et al. 238).

They identify these aspects as:
How the legacy can be traced through students beyond Oklahoma.
A turn toward embracing the locale while calling for more participatory design practice.
A material resourcefulness and environmental consciousness.
Experiment with organic forms.

Davis' work engages all four of these aspects to varying degrees. Although he designed and built projects across the United States, it is his northern California body of work – his response to its topography and ecosystem – that establishes his importance as a designer.

Davis' work was client centered. He chose clients as much as they chose him and they became friends for life. Nancy Barbour recounts that he not only designed their house, chose the furnishings, but also told her what she should wear.

Davis' material resourcefulness, particularly in the period of "wood expressionism" centered on an exploration of the possibilities of wood construction.

In comparing Davis' work to Goff and fellow students such as Greene and Muennig, one might be tempted to say that he was less interested in organic forms, but this is to misunderstand what Davis was doing with structure. In the archive of his work, now at the University of Oklahoma, is a design for a beer garden which was a student project. This project which has many of the hallmarks of the organic design typical of the school at that time, also shows the emphasis of repetitive structure and the strong relationship between interior and exterior space which would characterize his work.

Davis complemented these ideas with the strong controlling device of singular roof forms. His work plays a balancing act between conservative and radical.

Davis' life was one of dualities, beginning with his upbringing in Oklahoma and his maturity in California. His Episcopalian conservatism and his homosexual reality, his love of architecture and his love of landscape architecture. Artists seek to explore, reconcile and exploit such dualities. This is clearly evident in his work.

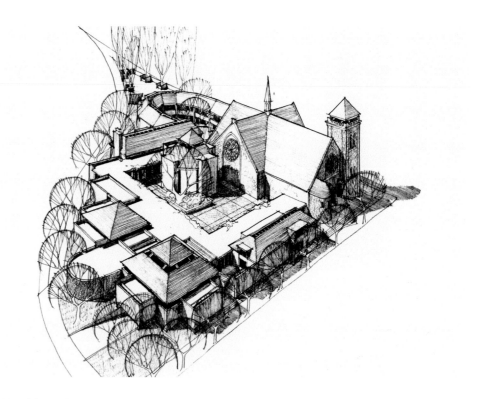

Above Charles Warren Callister, Addition to the First Unitarian Universalist Church. San Francisco, CA (1964-74). Entry to Courtyard and renderings by Warren Callister.

Davis' body of work – particularly that of his Wood Expressionist period mirrors Goff's interpretation of his reading of Stein's "continuous present" – each project is the result of his open-ended collaboration with the client, the spaces are multivalent and can transform themselves over time, because of the many layers of experience they provide.

Davis' work also exhibits the influence of architects who practiced in the First (1880s – early 1920s), Second (1928–1942) and Third Bay Tradition (1945 through the 1980s). The robust character of the buildings of Davis' wood expressionist period recall the work of Bernard Maybeck (1962–1951) who is seen as the founder of the First Bay Tradition. Its characteristics include an emphasis on craftsmanship, volume, form and asymmetry. Maybeck's dramatic redwood houses and the heavy timbered University of California Faculty Club with its magnificent large fireplace find their echoes in Davis' work. One need look only as far as the grand fireplaces in the houses he designed for himself during this period.

Donald MacDonald who worked with Davis in these early years recounted that Davis not only admired and visited Maybeck's work, but also admired the work of Warren Callister (1917–2008) who also practiced in Marin County. The concrete detailing and redwood trellises of Callister's projects including the First Unitarian Universalist Church in San Francisco find their echoes in Davis' work as well. Callister is considered a part of the Second Bay Tradition, even though his career extended through the Third. Davis should also be included in the Second Bay Tradition which is referred to as "Redwood Post and Beam" and has been defined as "a rustic, woodsy philosophy that was also informed by European modernism." In Davis' case, I would argue that it was informed more by Goff's pedagogy than European modernism.

Davis found his voice through a synthesis of many influences — his childhood in Oklahoma, his education at the University of Oklahoma, his time in Japan, and then his adopted home in Northern California with its own rich architectural traditions. Davis' designs are the result of his unique voice, a voice that was distinctly his own.

Sources

Greene, Herb. Mind & Image: An Essay on Art and Architecture. The University Press of Kentucky, 1976. p. 51, 69.

Guido, Luca, et al., editors. Renegades: Bruce Goff and the American School of Architecture. University of Oklahoma Press, 2020. p. 6, 7, 15, 22, 238.

Sullivan, Louis H. Kindergarten Chats and Other Writings. Wittenborn, Schultz, 1947. p. 164.

WOOD EXPRESSIONISM 1962–1979

174 HARRISON RESIDENCE

SAUSALITO, CALIFORNIA | 1962

In the early 1960s, Davis acquired a large lot at the western end of Sausalito between Bulkley and Harrison Avenues adjacent to the Catholic rectory. By donating a third of the property to the city for a playground, he was able to subdivide the remaining property into two lots. He built the house at 174 Harrison for himself and built 199 Bulkley for his sister and his soon-to-be brother in law who was serving in the Navy at the time.

174 Harrison was not only Davis's home, but his architectural office and calling card. The house exhibits a synthesis of the various influences and themes that he would continue to explore throughout his career. As an officer in the Navy (1955–1957), Davis travelled to Asia and his time spent in Japan was clearly formative.

Upon arriving at the entry court, one perceives a simple single-story Japanese pavilion structure, which belies the fact that this is actually a three-story home. The roof form dramatically holds the volume and the strong horizontal lines guide the eye to the view of Richardson Bay beyond. All of this is evident in the perspective view Davis created prior to construction.

One enters off the east-facing porch through a dramatic wall of glass doors – painted in what would become his signature blue (there are various accounts of the formulation of this paint color — one of which is Benjamin Moore Philipsburg Blue) — and into a grand paneled and beamed hall of dark oiled wood. The space is divided into a dining room to the south and a living room and study to the north, and is anchored by a fireplace/stair mass which connects the three floors of the house. The dining room, entry, and extension of the living room out to the view constitute a slot of space that actually begins on the deck above the garage – creating a sense of grand space – another theme that he would continue to explore. In addition to the strong influences of Japanese design and Frank Lloyd Wright, the living room echoes elements of the work of Bernard Maybeck's homes in Berkeley.

A bedroom/bath and galley kitchen complete the main floor of the house. Throughout his career, Davis would explore various configurations of this galley kitchen. The narrow spiraling stair that continues around the chimney mass counterpoints the scale of the open pavilion with a sense of mystery. The stair leads down to the lower level of the house with its two bedrooms and large recreation room. This room has large folding doors that open out to the lower yard. The blue Heath tile floor extends from inside to out. This was originally Davis' office and drafting room.

The master bedroom is located on the third floor within the roof form of the house with views out to the west toward Mount Tamalpais while the master bathroom offers views of Richardson Bay to the north.

Opposite page East elevation, 174 Harrison.

A RESIDENCE FOR 174 HARRISON AVENUE ∘ SAUSALITO, CALIFORNIA 4

Above Perspective showing house overlooking Richardson Bay.

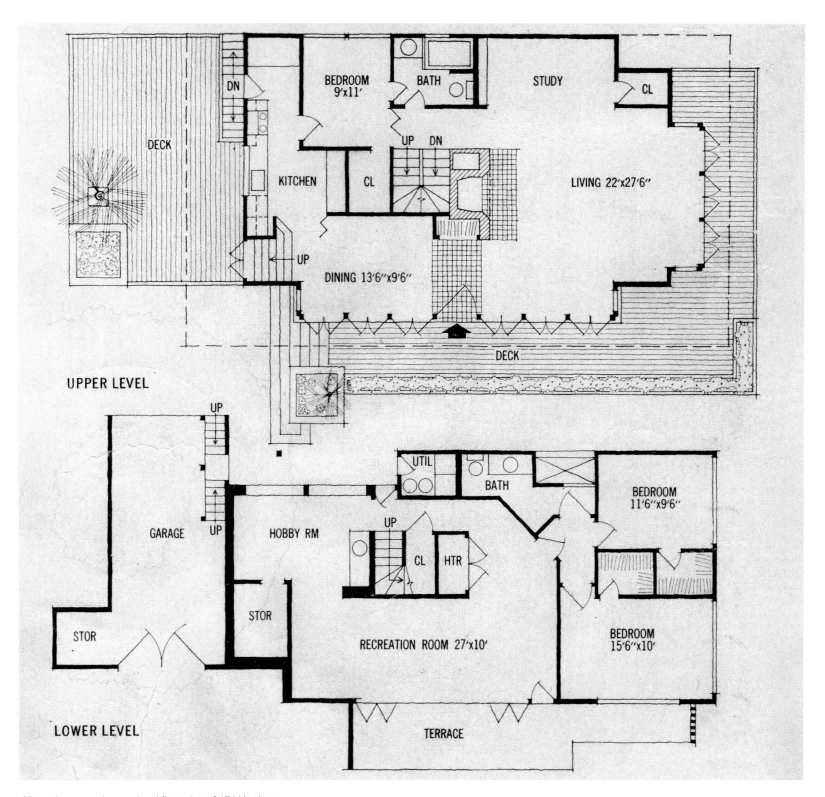

DECK

BEDROOM 9'x11'

BATH

STUDY

CL

DN

KITCHEN

CL

UP DN

LIVING 22'x27'6"

UP

DINING 13'6"x9'6"

DECK

UPPER LEVEL

UP

UP

GARAGE

HOBBY RM

UP

UTIL

BATH

BEDROOM 11'6"x9'6"

CL

HTR

STOR

STOR

RECREATION ROOM 27'x10'

BEDROOM 15'6"x10'

TERRACE

LOWER LEVEL

Above Lower and upper level floor plan of 174 Harrison.

Above left East elevation featured on the cover of *California Home Magazine*. **Above right** View of Richardson Bay from living room, photo from *California Home Magazine*. **Opposite page** View of living room fireplace, photo from *California Home Magazine*.

Opposite page Lower level garden room – this space was used by John Marsh Davis to house his office during the early years of his architectural practice. Featured in *California Home Magazine*. **Above** Contemporary photo of lower garden room looking out to the Bay.

"Throughout his career, Davis would explore various configurations of this galley kitchen. The narrow spiraling stair that continues around the chimney mass counterpoints the scale of the open pavilion with a sense of mystery."

—

Above Entry showing garage under deck, photo from *California Home.* **Right** East elevation.

BARBOUR RESIDENCE

KENTFIELD, CALIFORNIA | 1965

The Kentfield residence that Davis designed for Nancy and Donald Barbour sits on a dramatic, oak-filled site above a ravine. Nancy Barbour found Davis as the result of seeing 174 Harrison Avenue published in *California Home Magazine.* She recounts that when she went to meet him he said that he was not sure that he was the architect for her – perhaps this was a test – but out of it emerged a lifelong friendship with the Barbour family and several amazing projects.

Like 174 Harrison, the Barbour Residence expresses itself as a singular rectangular pavilion. The main public floor is located at the middle, with bedroom floors above and below. The hillside site created the opportunity to arrive across a pedestrian bridge on the south side of the house. In an early sketch, Davis explored the idea of this bridge going over a large swimming pool. Perhaps he recognized that this was an extravagance that was prohibitively expensive in that he also included a Roll's Royce in the foreground in this sketch.

The garden that replaced the pool was designed by noted California landscape architect Thomas Church. From the bridge, one is given a dramatic view of the east side of the house. The exterior siding is a version of Redwood board and batten that accentuates the notion of a wood framed house. The vertical proportions are extended into the two gigantic sliding glass doors that connect the garden and living room. Early schemes explored three and five bay versions with swinging doors.

The entry experience is one of compression – one stands at the southeast corner of the house in the dark small entry vestibule looking down the long length of the sliding doors – light flooding in from the east – you are pulled downward to the main living level – even though the stairs to the upper level are right beside you. Davis studied this space in great detail, as is shown in the perspectives included here. These perspectives show Davis exploring the fireplace mass at the center of the house (similar to 174 Harrison) prior to the final solution, which pushed it to the west wall. Note that even in the scheme with the fireplace first shown on the west, the large room is not yet partitioned with the bookcase that would create the symmetrical composition of living area flanked by kitchen/dining (north) and music room (south).

The fireplace is of a truly grand scale. Davis paid great attention to fireplaces, often designing unique hanging hooks such as the one he did here. One is drawn into the dining/kitchen area to the north of the living room by the rhythm of the west-facing windows that continue uninterrupted along with the window bench. The same is true of the music room on the south. The sill of the windows provides the back of the bench and this line extends to become the railing on the South deck. Both decks feature large doors that dissolve the line between interior and exterior space. This dissolving of separation is dramatically extended on the north wall of the kitchen where shelving is backed by a large single pane of glass rather than a solid wall.

Opposite page Great indoor outdoor living room.

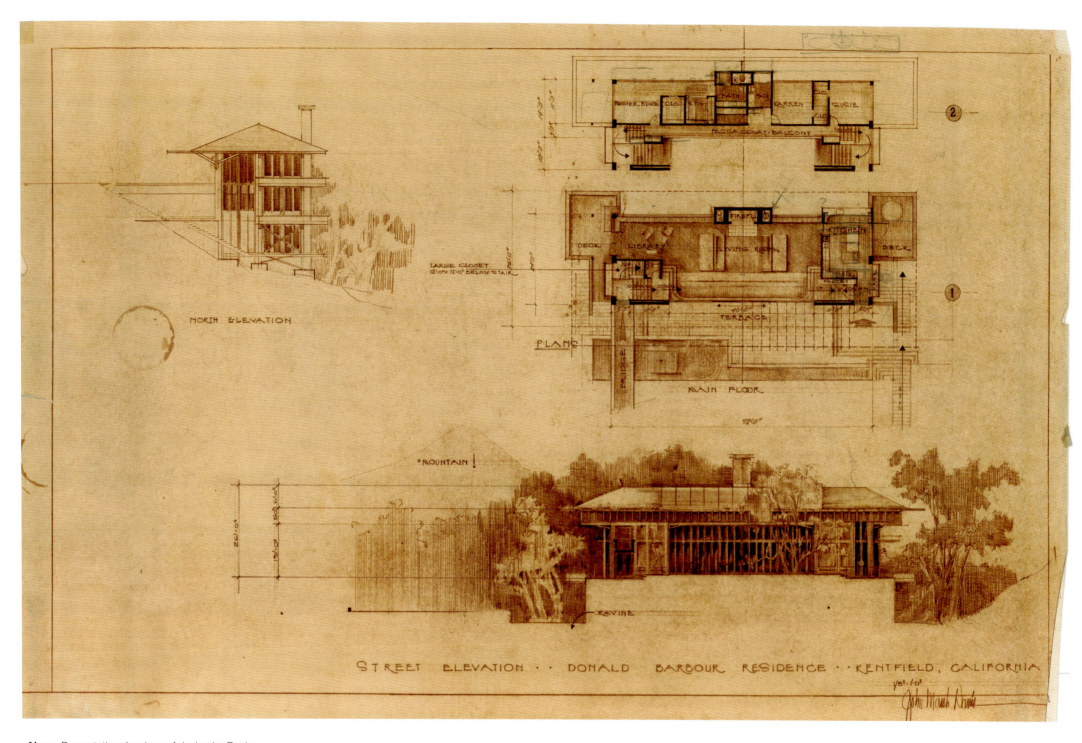

NORTH ELEVATION

LARGE CLOSET
12'-0" x 12'-0" BELOW STAIR

PLANS

MAIN FLOOR

MOUNTAIN

RAVINE

STREET ELEVATION · · DONALD BARBOUR RESIDENCE · KENTFIELD, CALIFORNIA

Above Presentation drawings of design by Davis.

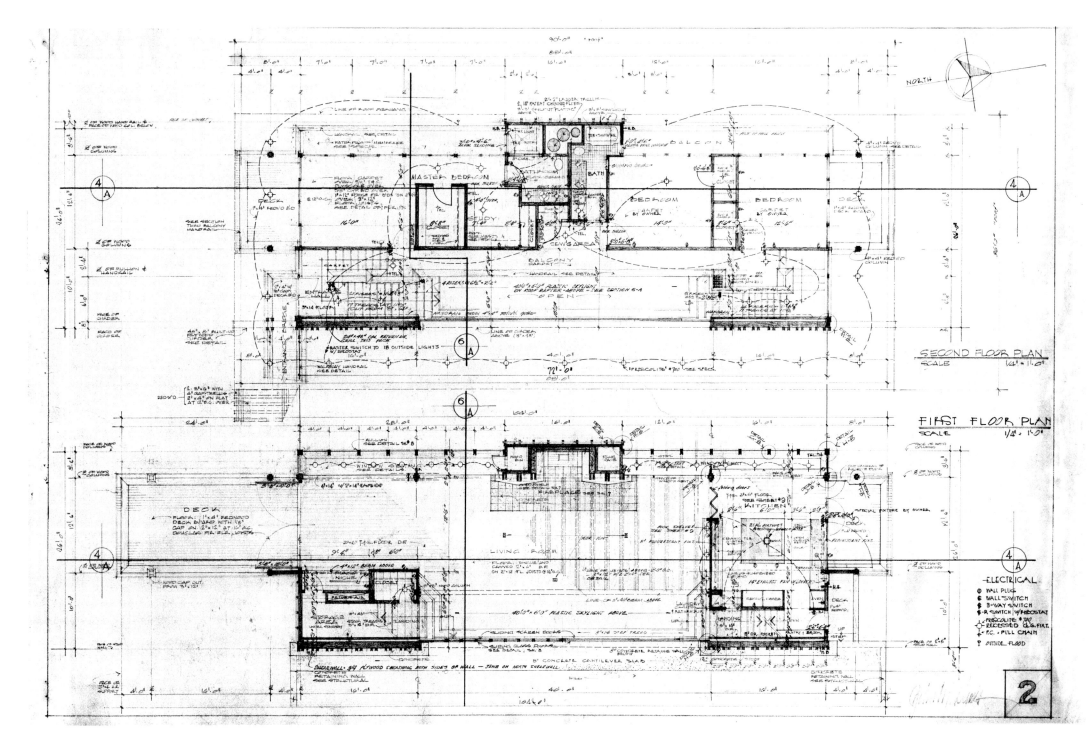

Above Main floor and upper floor plan.

Davis designed homes for entertaining. To this end, he designed three tables that could be put together to form a single large table in the Barbour living room to host large dinner parties. Nancy Barbour recounts having 41 for Christmas. Davis's 50th birthday was also celebrated here.

Davis was instrumental in the furnishing of the spaces he designed, insisting here on the McGuire Campaign chairs and white sofas and Japanese vases and Oriental carpets. From time to time Davis would visit the Barbours and decide to change something about the house, on one occasion deciding to remove some trim detail from the wooden ceiling beam. In many of his client's homes, as is the case here, he furnished the exterior patios and decks with Walter Lamb bronze patio chairs and chaise lounges. His discerning vision extended into the fashion of his clients, as Nancy Barbour tells that he would state his approval or disapproval of what she was wearing.

The entry stair on the south side of the house is mirrored by a stair on the north. Just as the space of the living room extends into the dining and music rooms, here the space extends up to the second floor. This quality of interweaving is accentuated by the horizontal stairs extending into the bookcases.

The stairs lead up to the interior bridge, which overlooks the eastern space and its sliding doors opening onto the garden. From here the Barbours can view their guests arriving across the bridge. Three bedrooms open to the west off of this bridge. The north stair also connects to the lower level where an additional bedroom is located.

The south-facing master bedroom deck features dramatic views of Mt. Tamalpais. The deck supports dissolve into a Wisteria-clad trellis structure, a signature of many Davis projects. The bracketed treatment of the roof overhangs make this trellis an emphatic part of the house, both celebrating structure and dematerializing the walls holding up the roof, thus creating the feeling of the roof floating above.

Davis's interest in playing with notions of dematerialization is also seen in his use of mirrors. An example at the Barbour Residence is the mirror that extends garden path seen from the music room deck, giving the sense that it meanders beyond the boundary of the property. Davis would go on to use mirrors to skillfully extend space in many projects, including his own home at 96 Santa Rosa in Sausalito.

Opposite page View to garden through great sliding doors.

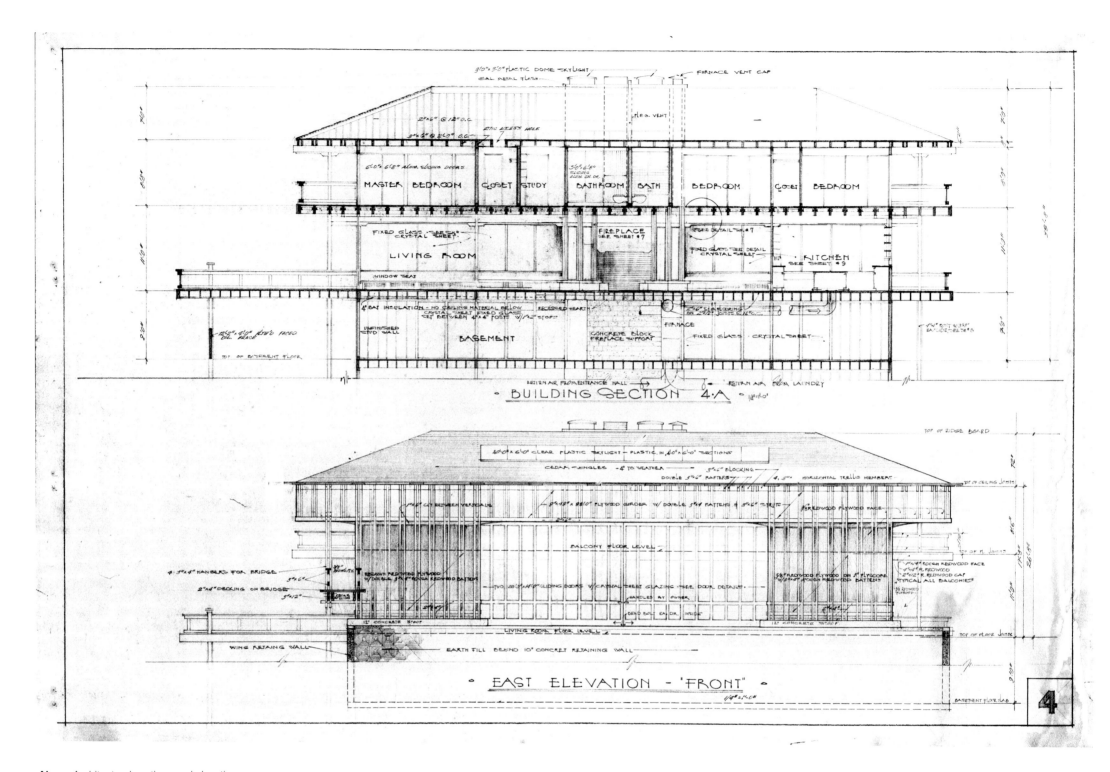

Above Architectural sections and elevations.

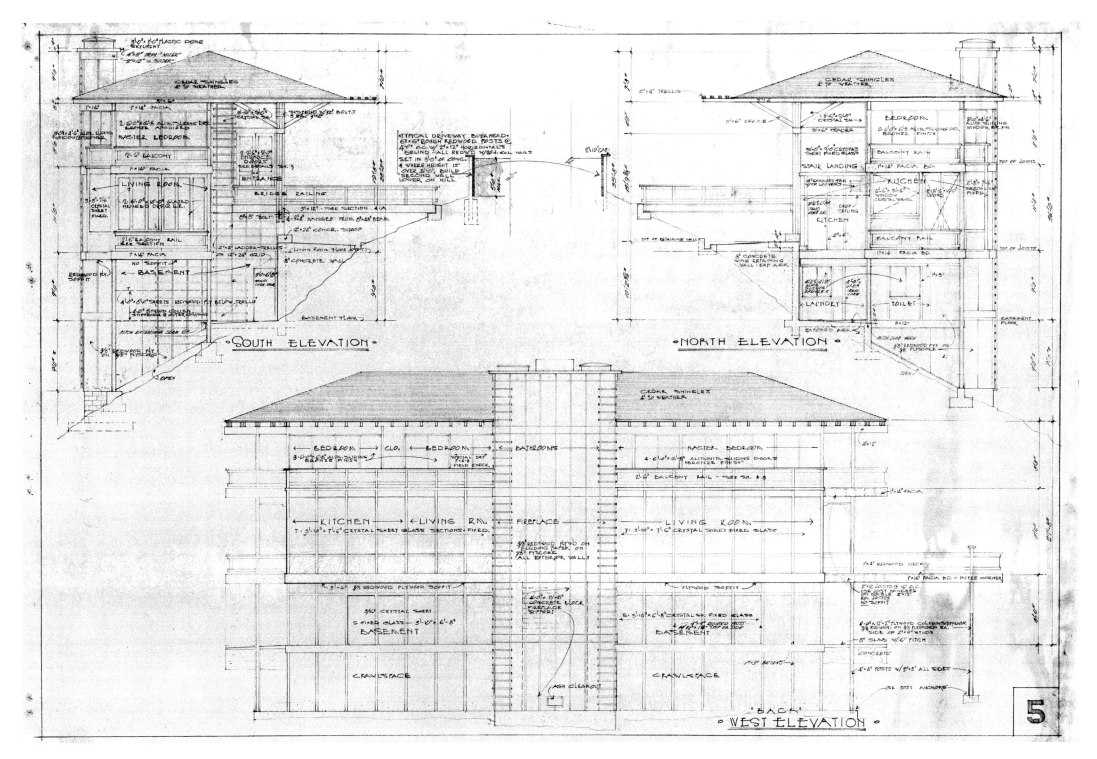

Above Architectural elevations.

Above Barbour Residence under construction. **Opposite page left** Construction team, Nancy Barbour and John Marsh Davis. **Opposite page right** John Marsh Davis inside the Barbour House construction side.

Opposite page Looking up the stairs. **Above top** Design study of eastern hall with alternate fireplace location. **Above** View looking from entry. **Right** View looking from entry to living room from the bottom of the stairs.

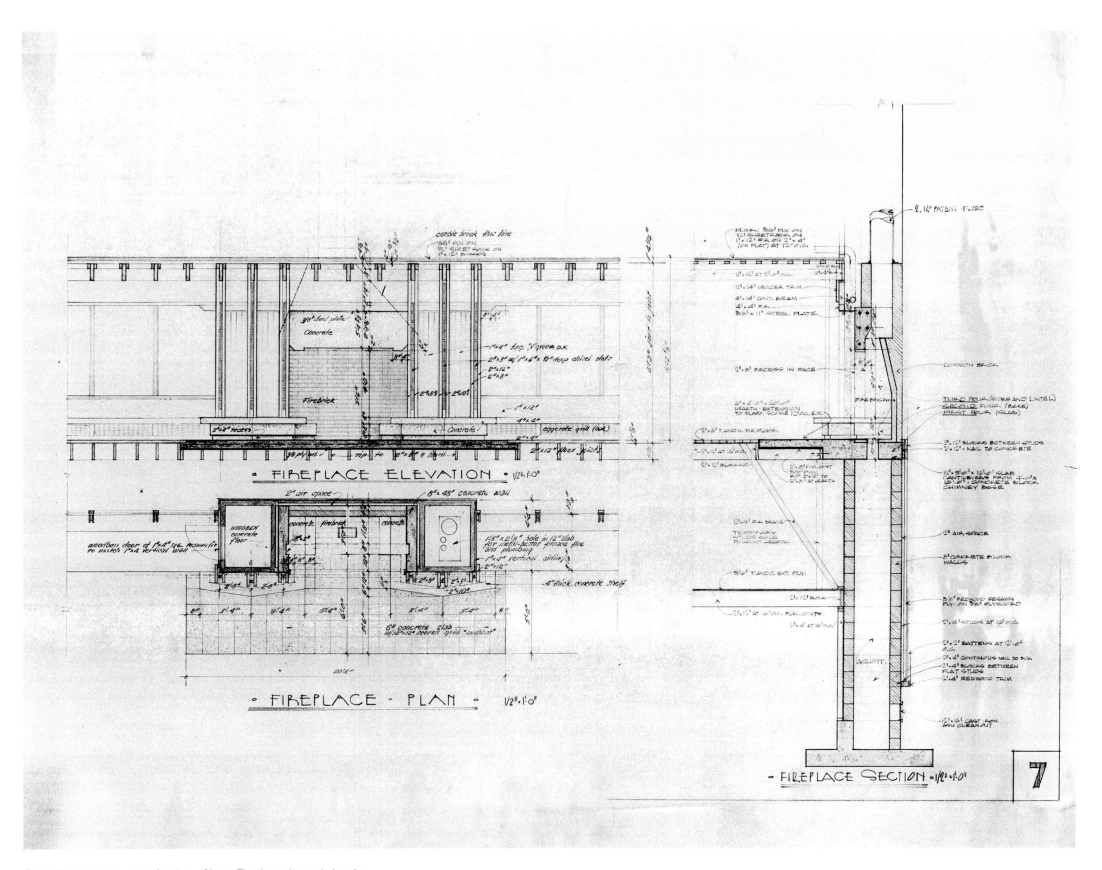

· FIREPLACE ELEVATION · 1/2"=1'-0"

· FIREPLACE - PLAN · 1/2"=1'-0"

· FIREPLACE SECTION · 1/2"=1'-0"

7

Opposite page Living room fireplace. **Above** Fireplace plan and elevation.

Opposite page View of kitchen and breakfast table with window bench. Note kitchen shelving in front of windows. **Above** Looking out through music room and onto deck with view of Mt. Tamalpais.

Above John Marsh Davis perspective drawing of design, showing entry bridge. **Opposite page** Nancy and Donald Barbour on the entry bridge to their home.

"Like 174 Harrison, the Barbour Residence expresses itself as a singular rectangular pavilion. The main public floor is located at the middle, with bedroom floors above and below. The hillside site created the opportunity to arrive across a pedestrian bridge on the south side of the house. ".

—

MUELLER RESIDENCE

BELVEDERE, CALIFORNIA | 1965 (DEMOLISHED)

The Mueller house consists of a strong gabled form that looks out from Belvedere Island to the Golden Gate Bridge. The main living level has a wrap-around porch and is anchored at its southern end by a grand fireplace. The northern end of the house has a cross gable set at ninety degrees and connects to the pool deck by means of ascending stairs.

Adolph Mueller was an important early client of John Marsh Davis, and would recommend him for other significant projects. Mueller was an attorney and served on the board of Souverain. Through this project, he provided the introduction to Joseph Phelps, founder of Hensel Phelps, the construction company hired to build the winery. Phelps would go on to hire Davis for his Stonebridge project, which would ultimately evolve into Joseph Phelps Vineyards.

Today, only the garage remains where the house once stood.

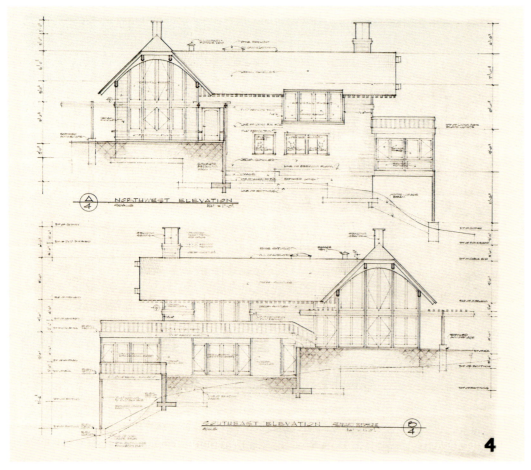

Above Northwest elevation and Southeast elevation. **Opposite page** Early photo of view from Bay-side deck into living room.

Above View of the living room.

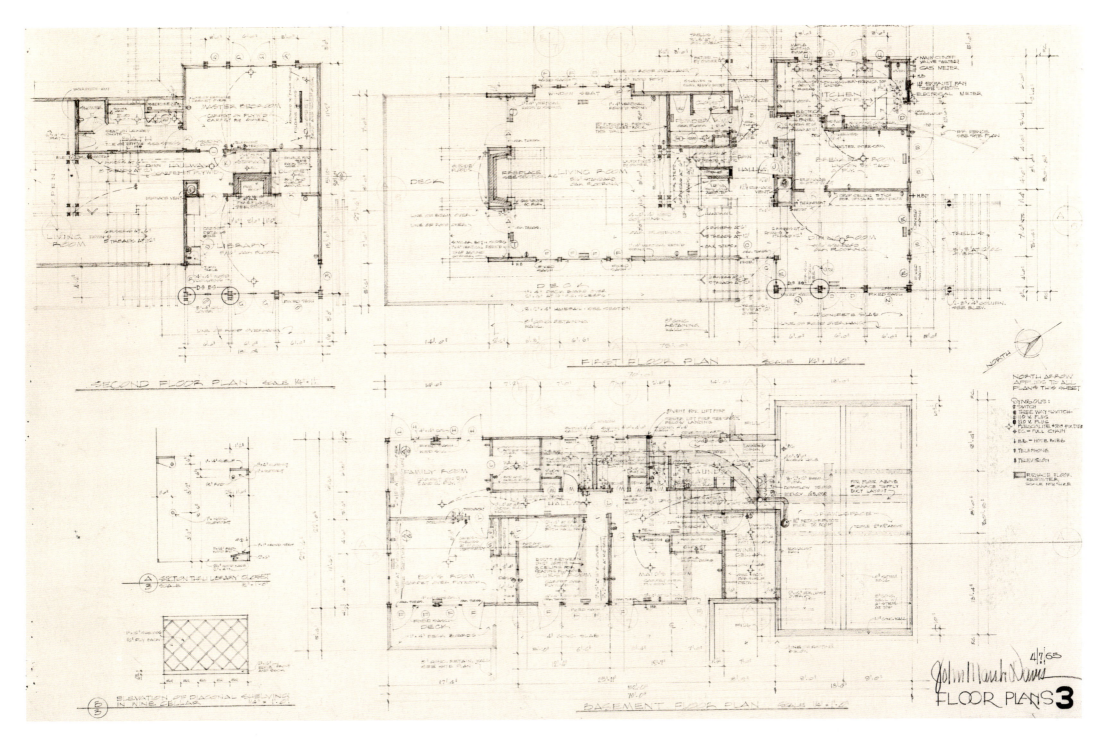

Above Architectural plans.

This spread Courtyard view.

Widen garage

Among John Marsh Davis drawings is this spectacular rendering for a house looking out over San Francisco Bay toward the Golden Gate Bridge in the distance. This is the view one gets from Belvedere Island and substantially the same view as from the Mueller House site. It is possible this was a preliminary study for the house – which seeks to draw all the programmatic elements under a single roof. This strategy is one found throughout Davis' work.

—

PERLOFF RESIDENCE

MILL VALLEY, CALIFORNIA | 1965 (UNBUILT)

The surviving drawings of the Perloff Residence show Davis' continued fascination with strong gabled forms. Here the main mass groups together primary living spaces in a double height volume with the bedroom wing tying into the center of the house and stairs connecting up to the children's bedrooms, which occupy the space above the library and master bedroom suite. Diagonal window bays in the north and south ends of the main mass create seating alcoves in the living room and a pantry and breakfast room off the kitchen.

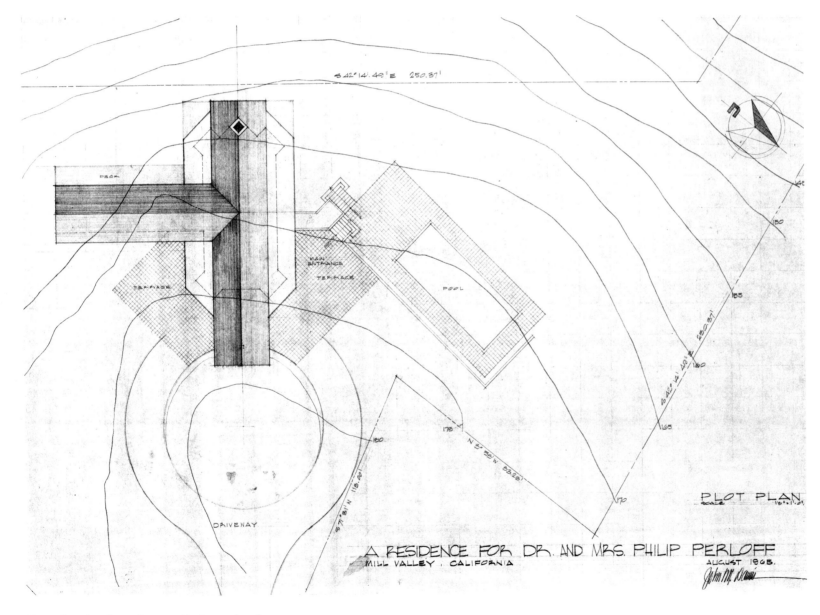

Above Site plan. **Opposite page** Northwest elevation.

NORTHWEST ELEVATION (POOLSIDE)
SCALE 1/4" = 1'.0".

A RESIDENCE FOR DR. AND MRS. PHILIP PERLOFF
MILL VALLEY, CALIFORNIA.   AUGUST 1965.

NEW TREES THIS WALL

- NORTHEAST ELEVATION — DRIVESIDE -

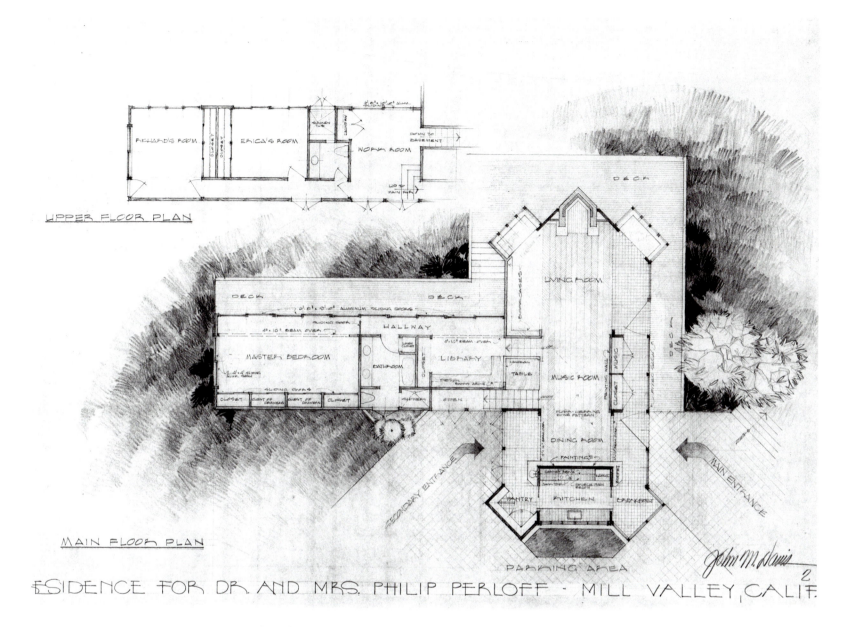

UPPER FLOOR PLAN

MAIN FLOOR PLAN

RESIDENCE FOR DR. AND MRS. PHILIP PERLOFF · MILL VALLEY, CALIF.

Opposite page Northeast elevation. **Above** Main floor plan.

"The surviving drawings of the Perloff Residence show Davis' continued fascination with strong gabled forms."

—

CALLE DEL SIERRA RESIDENCE

STINSON BEACH, CALIFORNIA | 1966

Davis built the Stinson Beach Residence for himself. The creation of the house right on the beach was a dramatic event for this small oceanfront community that was just beginning to see the development of vacation homes in the Sea Drift subdivision to the north. Davis chose to build within the small streets closer to town known as "calles."

The house is defined by its two-story hipped roof form that hovers over the ground floor. Glass corners on this ground floor accentuate the sense of the roof floating above the ground. Large central two-story dormers on the south, west, and north sides anchor the floating roof mass to the ground. The fireplace mass acts to do the same on the east side. The house is essentially a single large room that has two levels, and opens out onto a walled garden that surrounds the house. The front door is on the northeast corner.

Once again, Davis has you enter at the side of the building and orients you to the location of the stair which occupies this transparent corner. Straight ahead one encounters the grand east/west axis of the house with its tall doors opening at both ends out onto the garden. The living room framed by the three story structure of groups of four–10x10s is the heart of the house. The dining area with its view of the ocean to the west and inglenook fireplace to the north complete the space.

The house is at once monumental and relatively small in size, with each space opening into the next and the whole, the emphasis on both the axial and the diagonal.

This spread Photos from the beach. Early and contemporary.

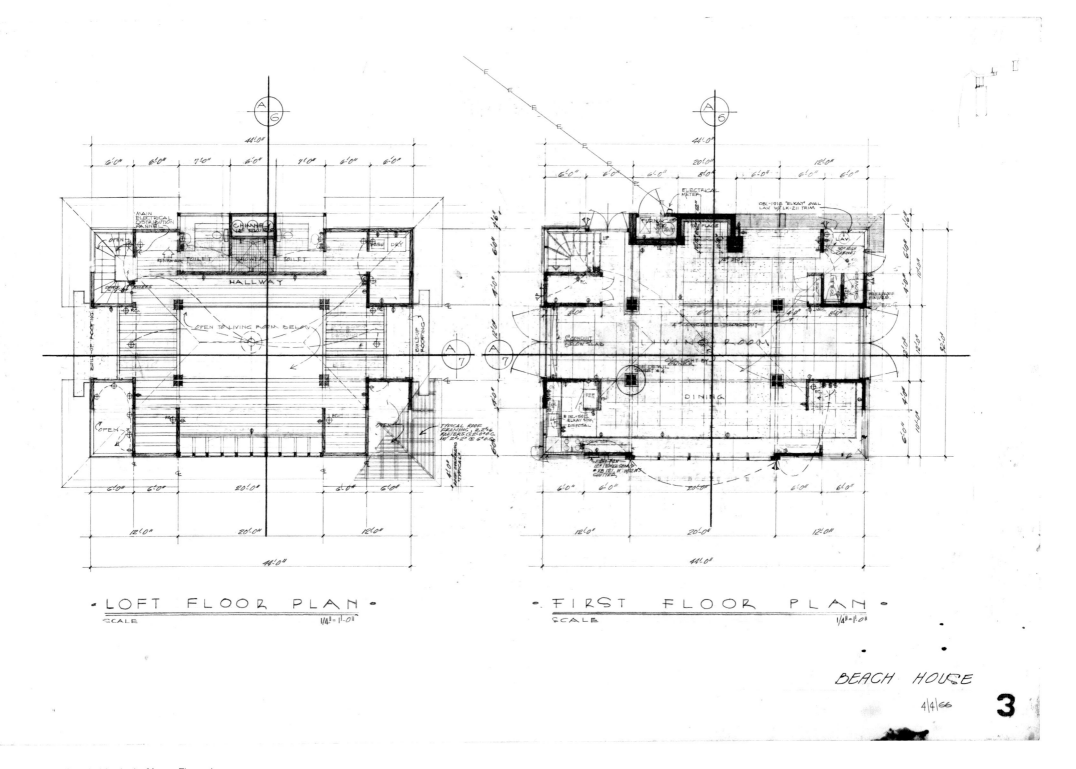

· LOFT FLOOR PLAN ·
SCALE   1/4"=1'-0"

· FIRST FLOOR PLAN ·
SCALE   1/4"=1'-0"

BEACH HOUSE
4/4/66

3

Opposite page Beachside deck. **Above** Floor plans.

Above Calle del Sierra under construction. **Opposite page** Early photos of Calle del Sierra.

Above View into kitchen from north side. **Opposite page** North side entrance to main living space.

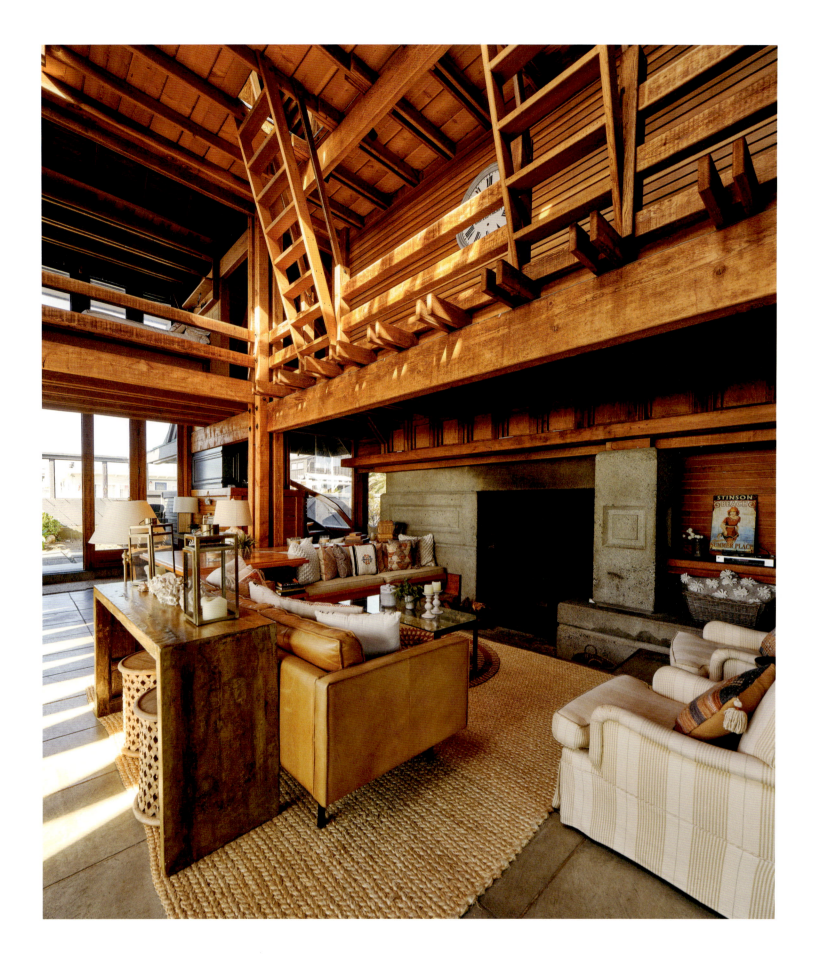

Opposite page Main living space looking toward the kitchen. **Right** Fireplace alcove to east.

Above left View through living area to dining area and beach beyond. **Above right** View of living area, showing fireplace and ladders from loft to upper level.

Above left View from east entrance through house. **Above right** View of dining area from east entrance.

" The creation of the house right on the beach was a dramatic event for this small oceanfront community that was just beginning to see the development of vacation homes in the Sea Drift subdivision to the north."

—

Opposite page Window bench/dining area on west wall looking into kitchen. **Above right** A tucked-away office with views toward the south. **Below right** View of kitchen.

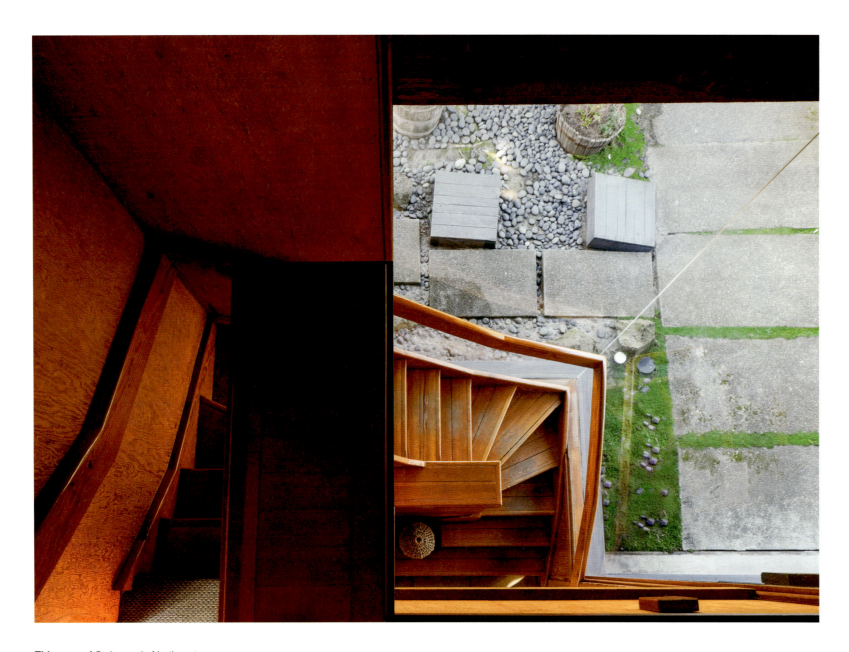

This spread Staircase in Northeast corner.

This spread The wrap-around loft floor has ladders to access the top floor and three open sleeping areas, all with Pacific Ocean views. Note shades to produce privacy.

Opposite page Ground floor bedroom with large sliding door that opens onto the east garden. **Above** The east garden. **Next spread** A landmark on Stinson Beach.

DUXBURY RESIDENCE

SEADRIFT SPIT, STINSON BEACH, CALIFORNIA | mid-1960s

In the archive of John Marsh Davis' drawings is this single undated sheet for a proposed oceanside residence for Mr. and Mrs. Herbert Drake on Seadrift Spit at Stinson Beach. Seadrift is a private enclave of houses at the far northwestern end of Stinson Beach which was developed by the Kent Family in the early 1960s. Many noted Bay Area architects designed ocean front houses in the development during this period of time and it is only natural that Davis would as well.

Duxbury shares themes that Davis explored at both 174 Harrison and at the Barbour residence. Here the short ends of the house face the street and the ocean and the long side of the house faces east with monumental glass doors opening out to the garden. As the prevailing wind blows from the west this would have been the sheltered side of the house. Similar to the Barbour House the fireplace is located opposite these glass doors on the west side of the house.

Given the absence of any other drawings for the house and the lack of a clear site plan it is not illogical to think of this elaborate drawing as a marketing effort that was sadly not successful. The house is similar to others if this period and for this reason is included here although there is no way to properly date it.

Davis loved Stinson Beach. It was both close to his home in Sausalito – no more than half an hour away but was a world away as well in that to get there one drives either over Mt. Tamalpais or on the dramatic coastal Highway One. He choose to build the Calle Del Sierra residence for himself in the old part of town on a site that gave him more freedom than in the architecturally regulated Seadrift development. When he later sold the Calle Del Sierra House he renovated a small house in the middle of town across from the Parkside Cafe.

Opposite page Aerial perspective of Duxbury Residence.

"DUXBURY"

AN OCEANSIDE RESIDENCE FOR
MR. AND MRS. HERBERT DRAKE ON
SEADRIFT SPIT, STINSON BEACH, CALIFORNIA

John Marsh Davis

BARNETT RESIDENCE

ST. HELENA, CALIFORNIA | 1966

The Barnett residence exhibits many of Davis' classic themes of the period. It is one of his first projects in the Napa Valley – built the same year as Clifford May's Robert Mondavi Winery, the seminal event from which the emergence of the "new" Napa Valley is often dated.

Davis designed a ground floor living space as a great trellised pavilion with a grand deck looking out across the grape-vines. The bedroom and kitchen spaces are modest, plywood-clad volumes on the uphill side of the site. The home is designed for entertaining and celebrating its place in the middle of Napa Valley, between forested slopes and expanses of vineyard. Davis would find Napa fertile ground for his work and for a while maintained an office in the Valley.

The Barnett Residence shows Davis' fascination with and debt to Japanese wood joinery, seen as well in his early Sausalito house. The residence also reveals his regard for the work of Bernard Maybeck, who reinterpreted the grand baronial halls of Europe in a uniquely California way. Davis distinguishes his work here through establishing the importance of the view and connection to the exterior.

Above Northwest elevation study. **Opposite page** Northwest elevation of Barnett Residence.

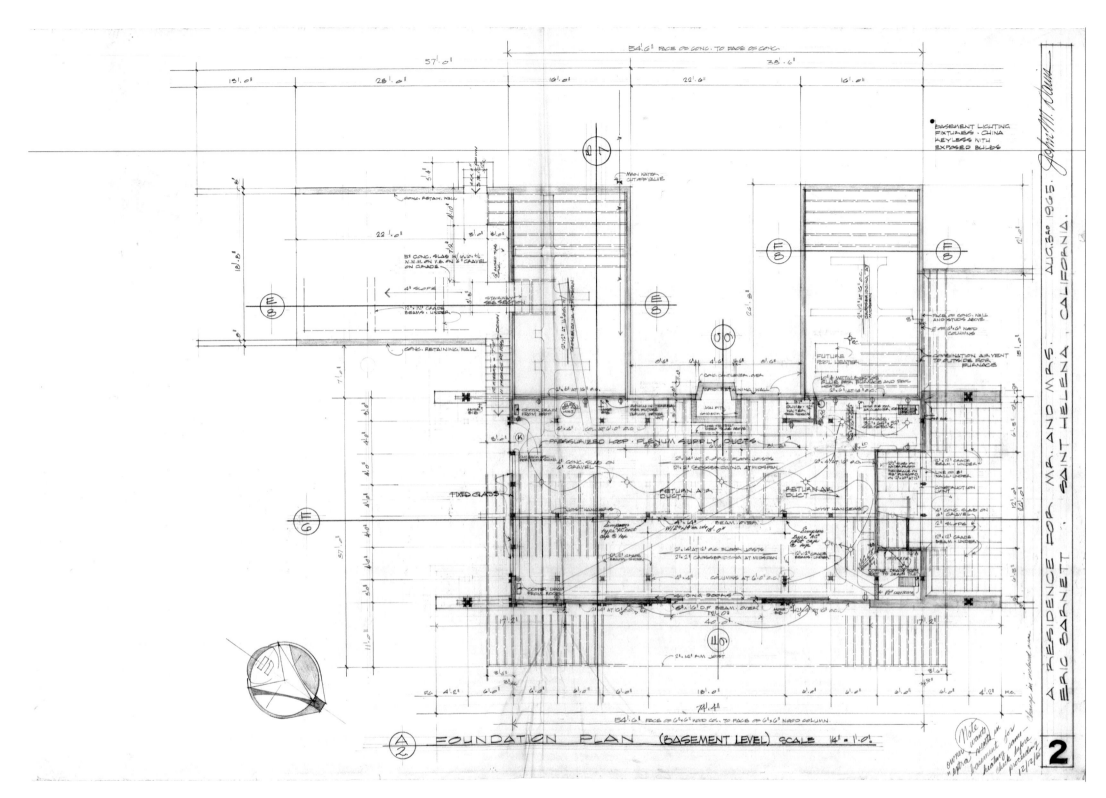

Above Foundation plan.

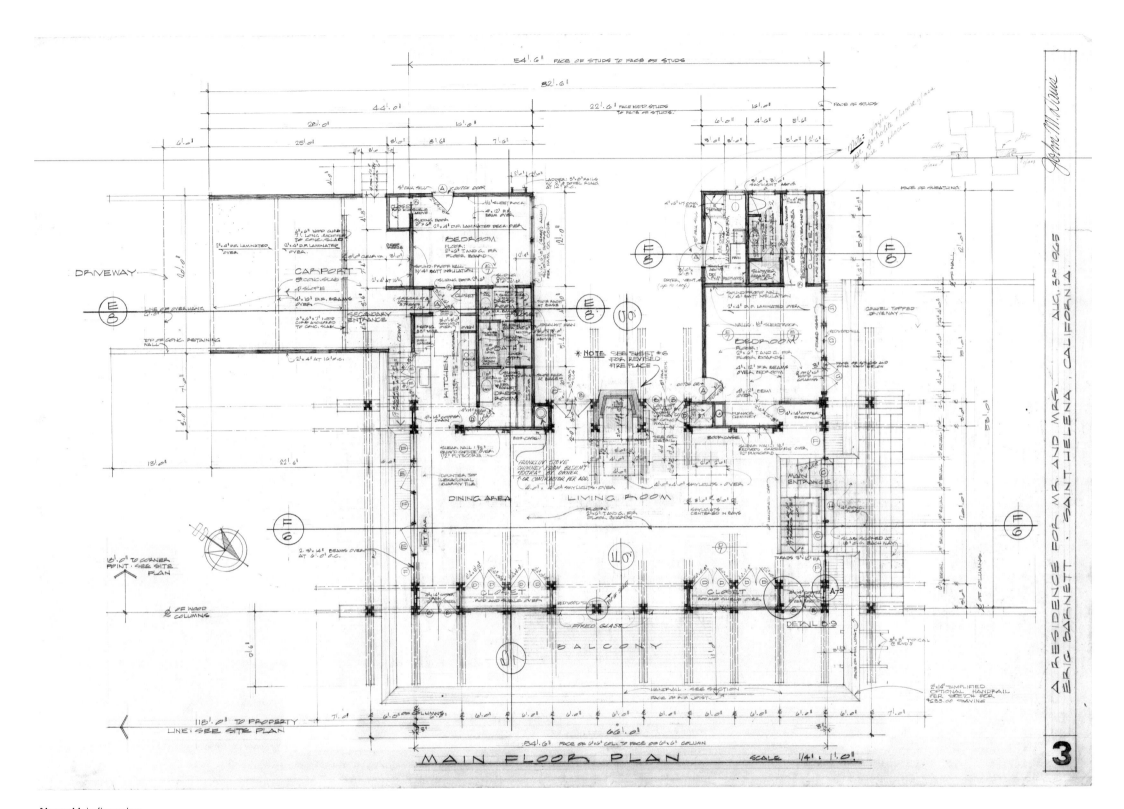

Above Main floor plan.

· NORTHEAST ELEVATION ·

· NORTHWEST ELEVATION ·

ERIC BARNETT RESIDENCE
ST. HELENA, CALIF.

Opposite page Northeast and northwest elevations studies. **Above** A photo shortly after construction taken by Davis. **Bottom** Construction photo showing the foundations of the house; Entry court with cars (note Davis' fascination with juxtaposing car and house).

"The residence also reveals his regard for the work of Bernard Maybeck, who reinterpreted the grand baronial halls of Europe in a uniquely California way."

—

Opposite page South east corner of the house. **Above** South elevation. **Bottom** Entry stair on north.

Above Main floor of the house and its deck float above the vineyard vines, offering panoramic views of Napa Valley.

Above On the western side, an intimate courtyard with a trellis that celebrates the vines.

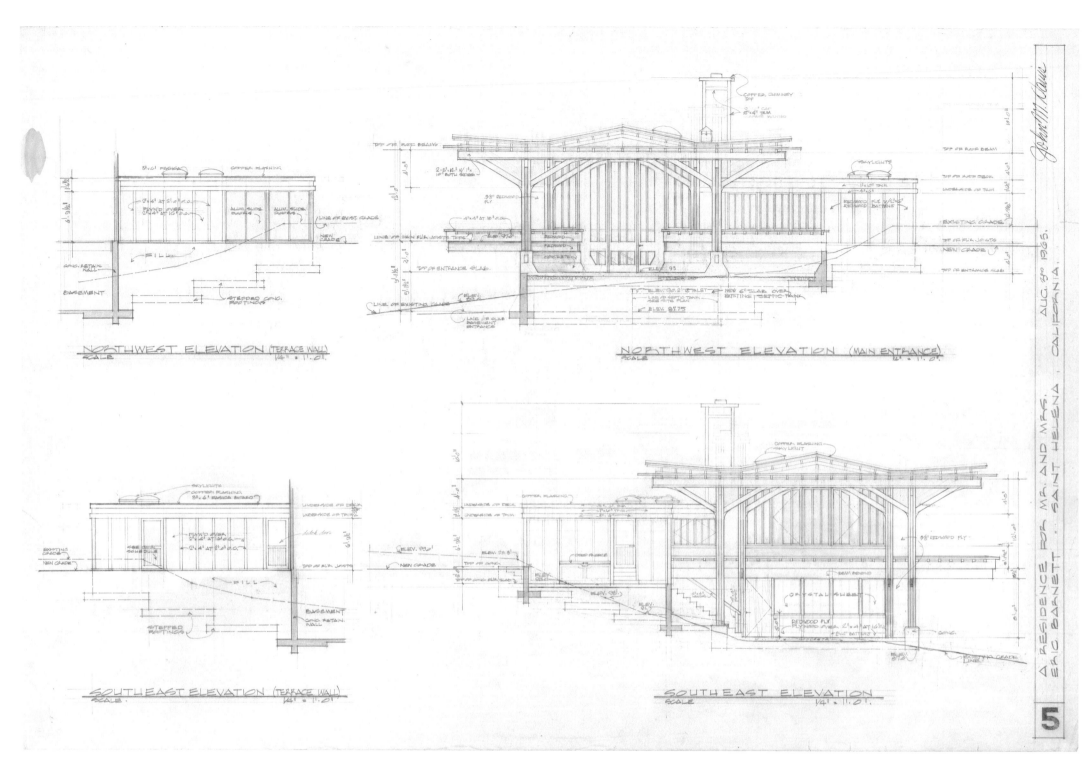

Above Elevations.

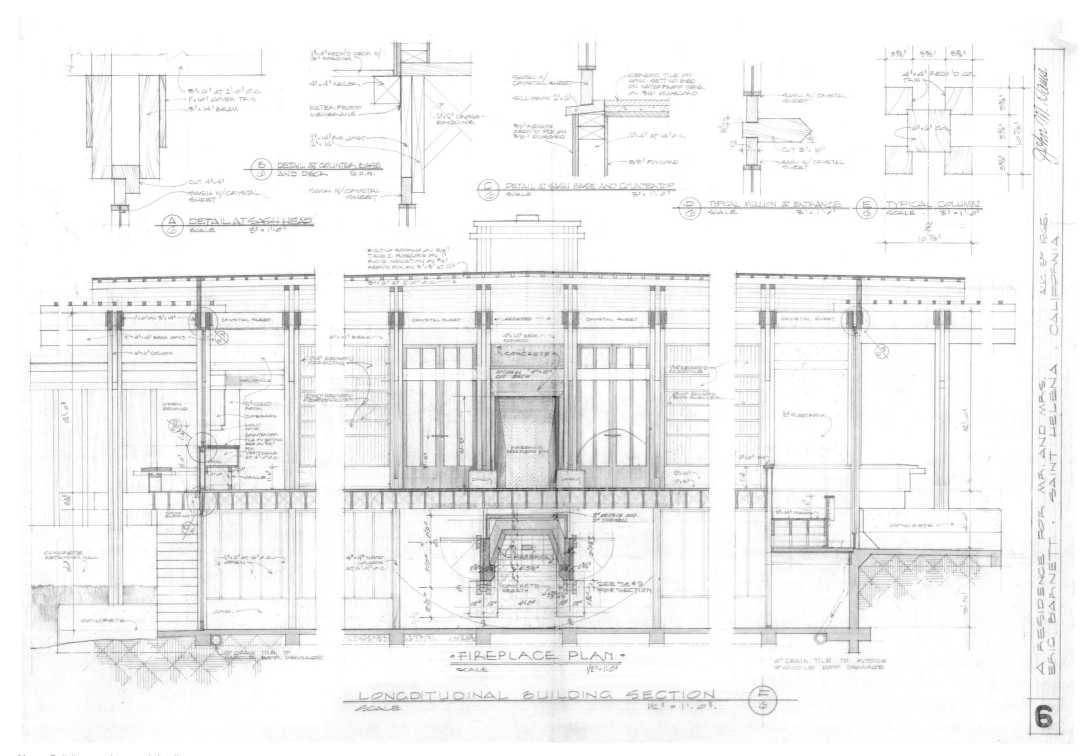

Above Building sections and details.

Above South end of great room. **Opposite page** Great room.

"WILOLOMLY"
STERLING RESIDENCE

MILL VALLEY, CALIFORNIA | 1969

The Sterling Residence explores many of the ideas present in Davis' work from the 1960s, including dramatic, overscaled spaces and the notion of a singularly powerful volume that is simultaneously composed of overlapping spaces and uses.

Here, a singular nave is both the entry and hall that organizes the house from the eastern front door to the western stair. The hall includes a flood-lit clerestory that shows off the structural rhythm of the house. The clerestory reveals itself to be a gigantic truss with the living room to one side and the dining room to the other. The house parallels the slope at the land, creating two distinct experiences with the dining room or north side opening onto terrace, and the living room or south side opening onto decks which overhang the floor below.

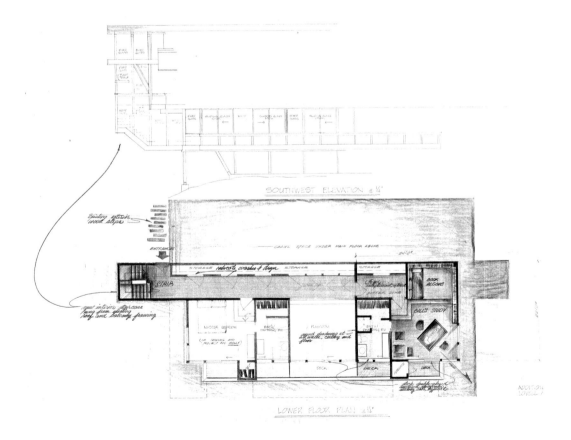

Above Study for lower floor plan. **Opposite page** Entry gates with trellis.

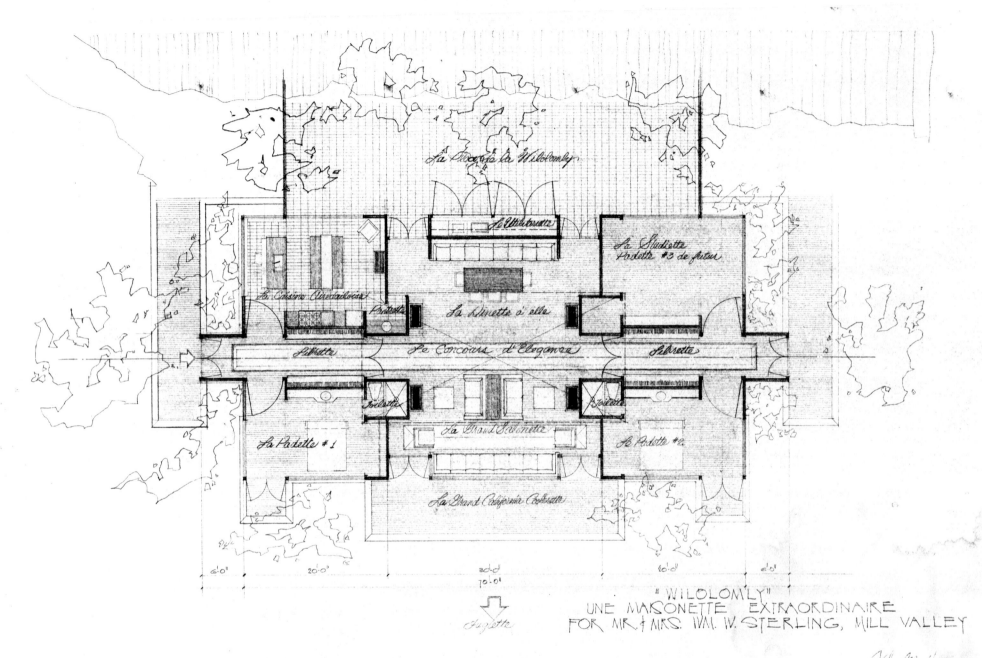

Above Study for main floor plan.

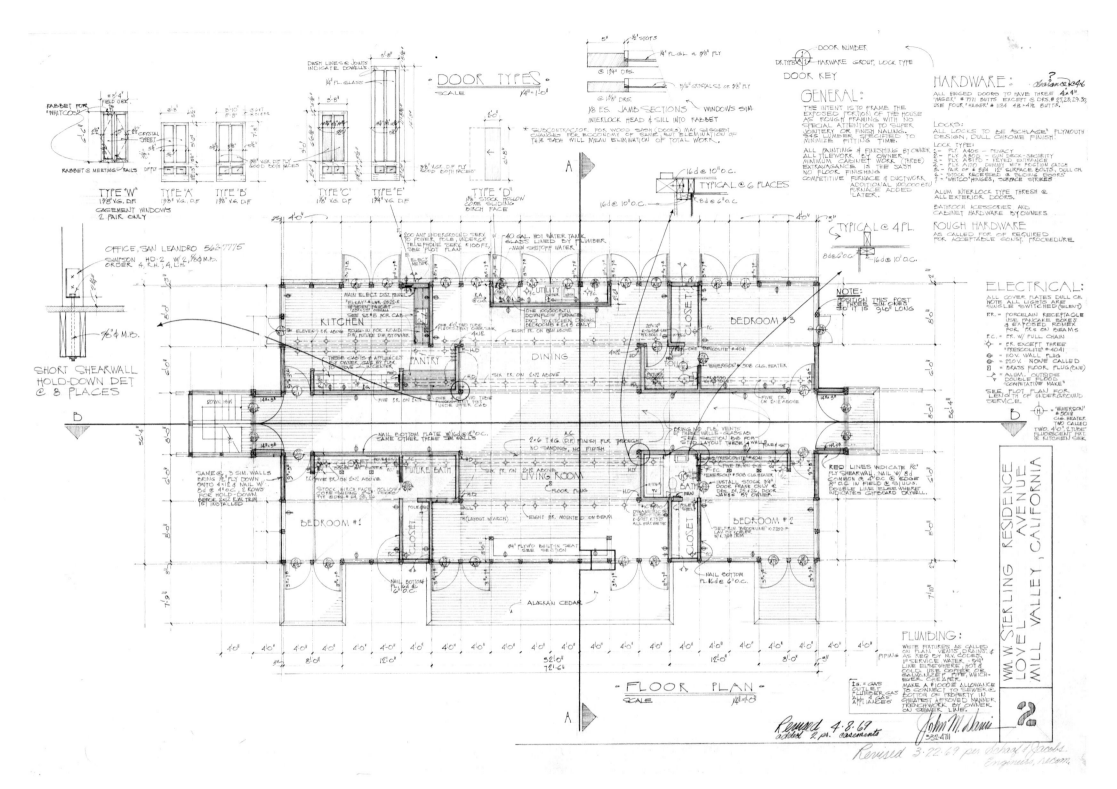

Above Main floor plan.

Above Living and dining areas on either side of central spire. **Opposite page** The central hallway is used as a library and has 16' high glass doors at each end.

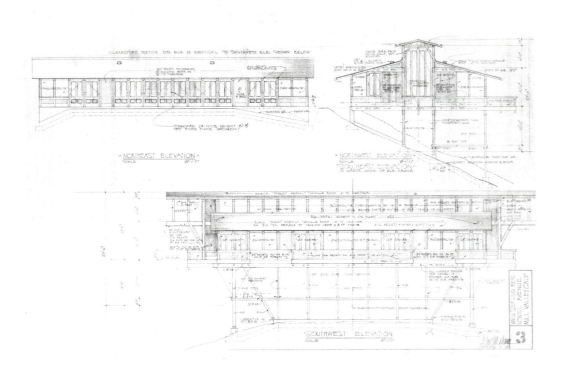

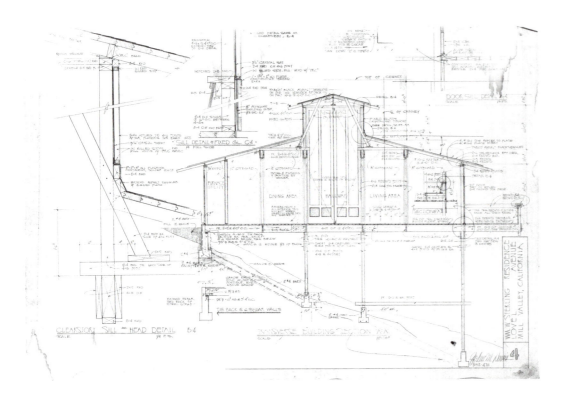

Above Building elevations and details. **Bottom** Building section and details. **Opposite page** Parking and gateway from the street leads to the terrace and kitchen.

ROUSH RESIDENCE

MEDINA, WASHINGTON | 1969 (NO LONGER STANDING)

The Roush Residence in Medina, Washington bears an interesting resemblance to Robert Creemer's Old Faithful Inn in Yellowstone National Park. His client, James Roush, had a great love of national park lodges so this was a logical starting point for this grand home.

Like so many of Davis' houses, the Roush Residence exploits its hillside location. The main living floor is in fact the second floor, which is entered on the uphill side and has a great deck on the lakeside. The bedroom floor is below this main floor, and above the ground level pool.

Loft spaces, occupying either end of the main living volume, and a widow's walk caps the roof of the house, accencuating the house as a grand volume to be explored.

Here the ground floor houses a large interior pool. A unique aspect of the house is that the rooms and dormers are all twisted by 45 degrees. The ground floor sliding doors that open the pool to the outdoors have proportions similar to the great sliding doors at the Barbour Residence.

Above Early presentation rendering that was later used for the invitation to the party celebrating the completion of the house. **Opposite page** West deck at second floor (principal living floor).

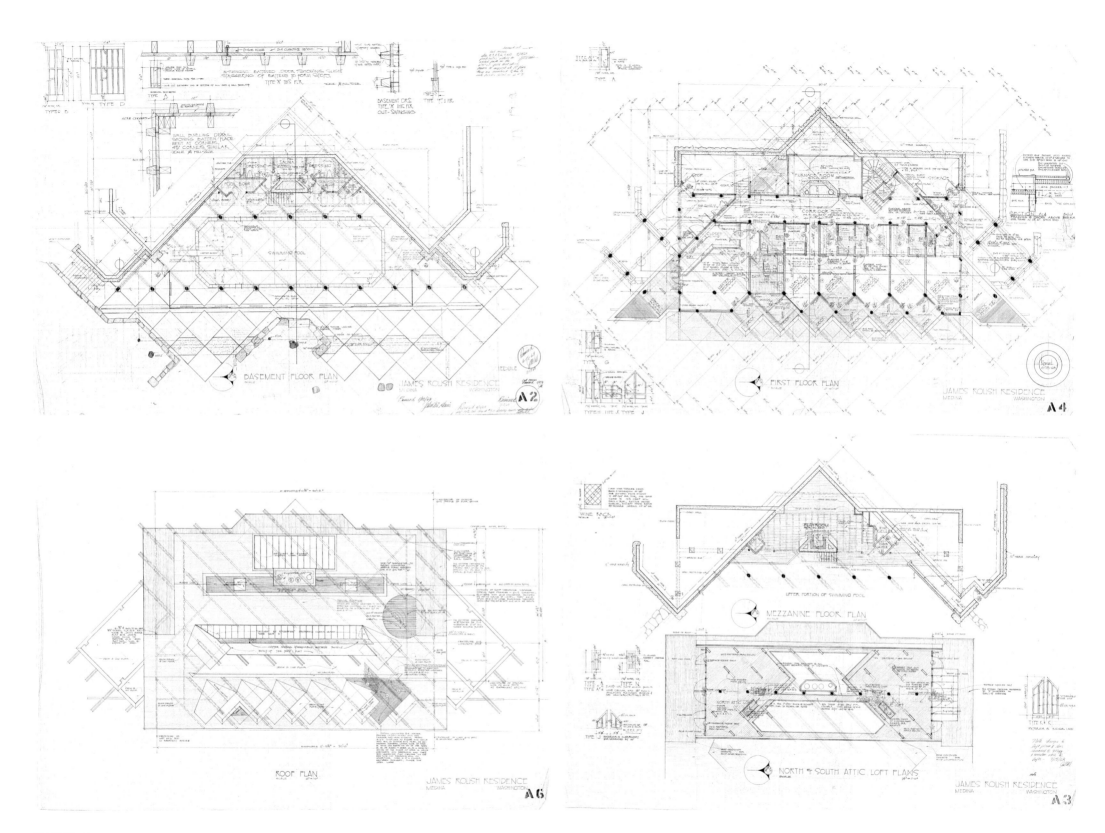

Above Plans.

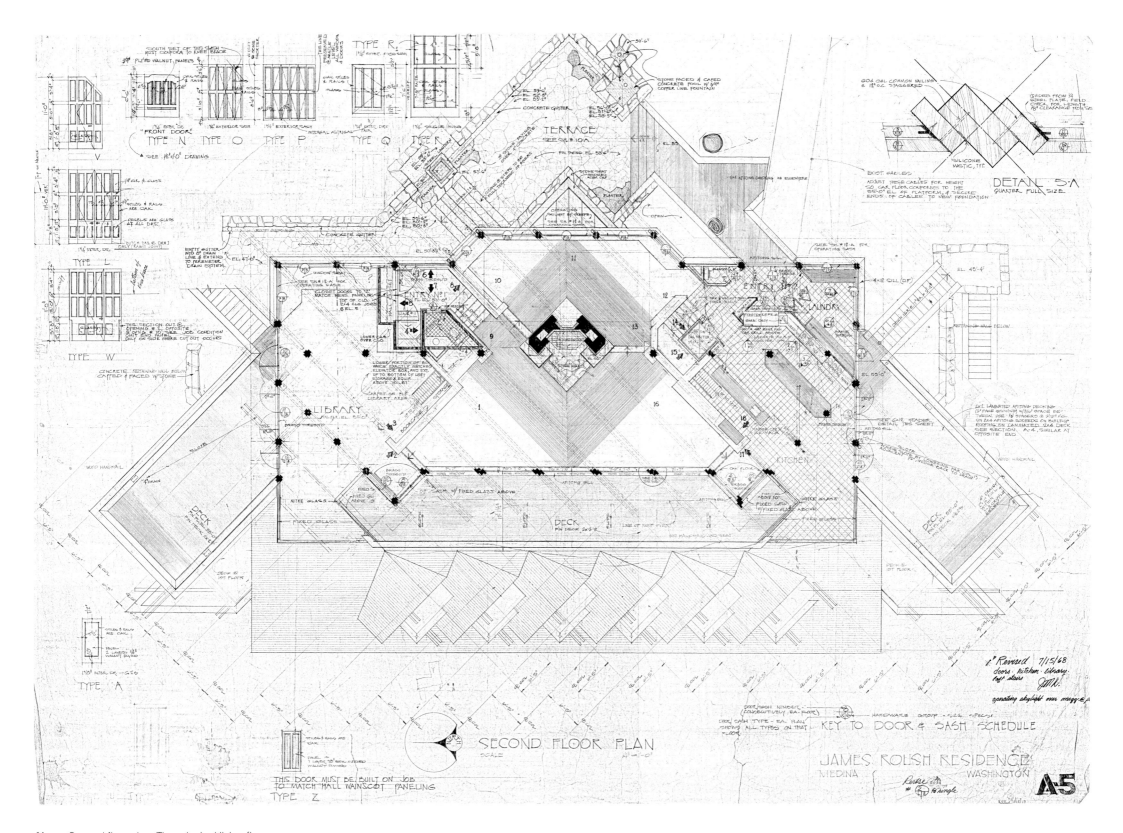

Above Second floor plan. The principal living floor.

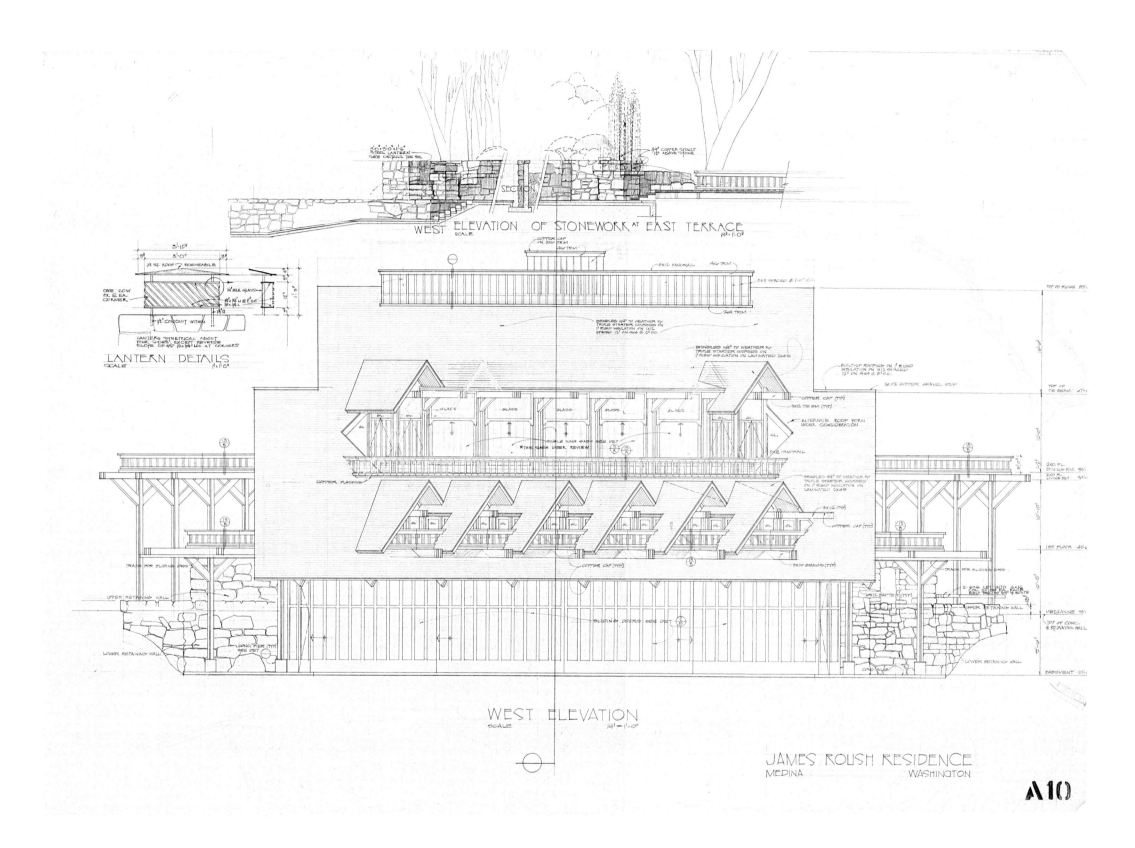

WEST ELEVATION OF STONEWORK AT EAST TERRACE
SCALE 1/4"=1'-0"

LANTERN DETAILS
SCALE 1"=1'-0"

WEST ELEVATION
SCALE 1/4"=1'-0"

JAMES ROUSH RESIDENCE
MEDINA   WASHINGTON

A10

Opposite page Construction photos showing relationship of the house to the lakeside. **Above** West, lakeside elevation.

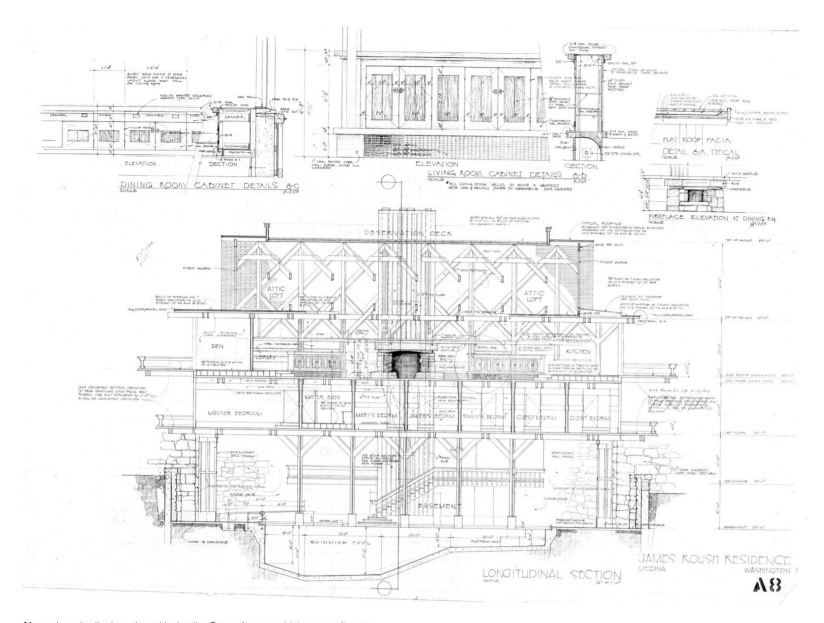

Above Longitudinal section with details. **Opposite page** Living room fireplace.

This spread Ground floor indoor pool.

"A unique aspect of the house is that the rooms and dormers are all twisted by 45 degrees. The ground floor sliding doors that open the pool to the outdoors have proportions similar to the great sliding doors at the Barbour Residence."

—

NASH RESIDENCE

BELVEDERE, CALIFORNIA | 1970 (SUBSTANTIALLY REMODELED)

The Nash Residence, like the Mueller House, is located on the south side of Belvedere Island with views toward Sausalito and the Golden Gate Bridge.

Here, Davis departs from a strategy of gathering all of the program under a single defining roof. The complex is created by three volumes that form a horseshoe around a central courtyard and pool. The main volume of the house is a grand double-height volume enclosed by a hipped roof. A central chimney mass defines the space, which has a cantilevered balcony running around it. The balcony links the two chimneys with the skylight that fills upper floor library space with light.

The chimney mass divides the house longitudinally – dining at the one end and living at the other. A sweeping deck extends all of these spaces out toward the Bay. Davis was able to juxtapose the built structures with the perfect world of the architectural courtyard to the north of the house and the dramatic San Francisco Bay to the south.

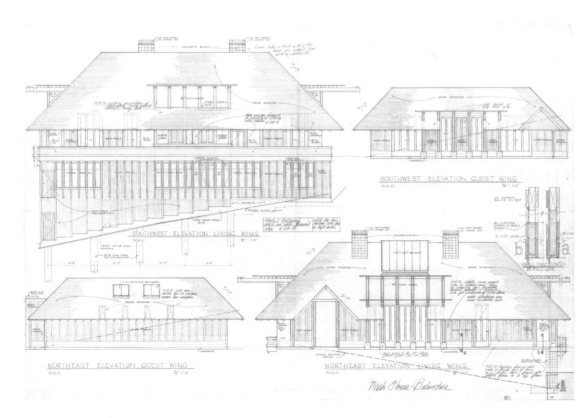

Above Elevation. **Opposite page** Aerial view.

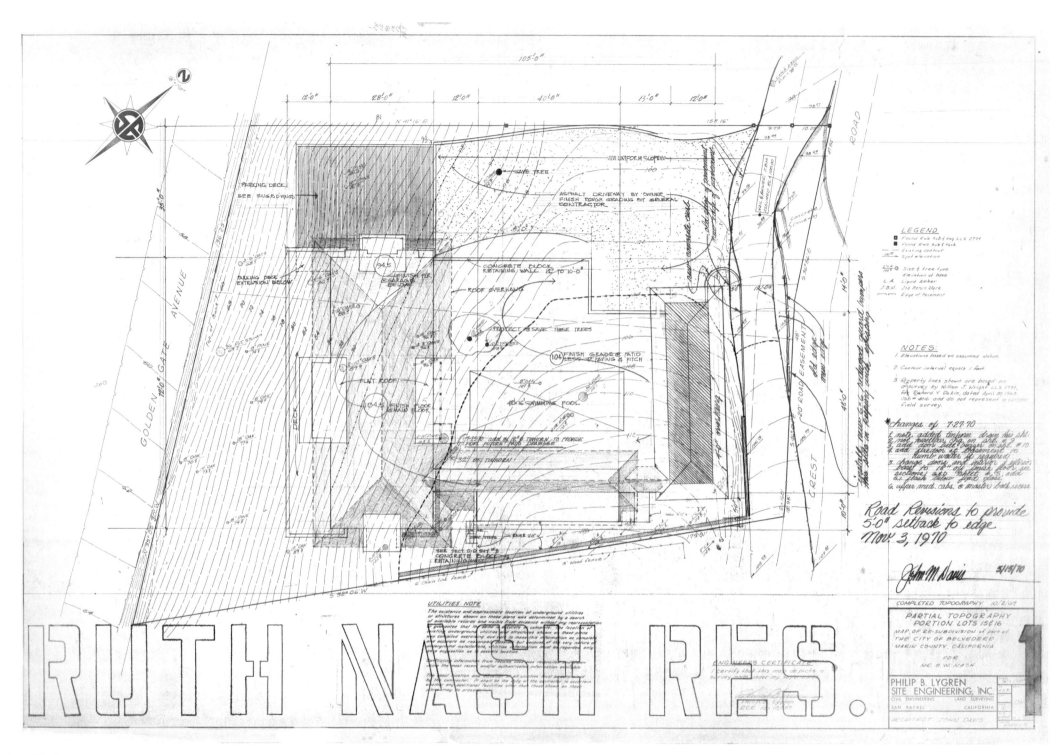

Above Site Plan.

Above Floor plan

Above Southwest corner of house with view of bay. **Bottom** West view of main living space looking toward courtyard. **Opposite page** View looking south toward bay.

Above Southwest deck with view of Mt. Tamalpais. **Bottom and right** Kitchen view looking toward San Francisco Bay.

Above Entry gallery looking toward pool. **Opposite page** Entry gallery.

"The complex is created by three volumes that form a horseshoe around a central courtyard and pool."

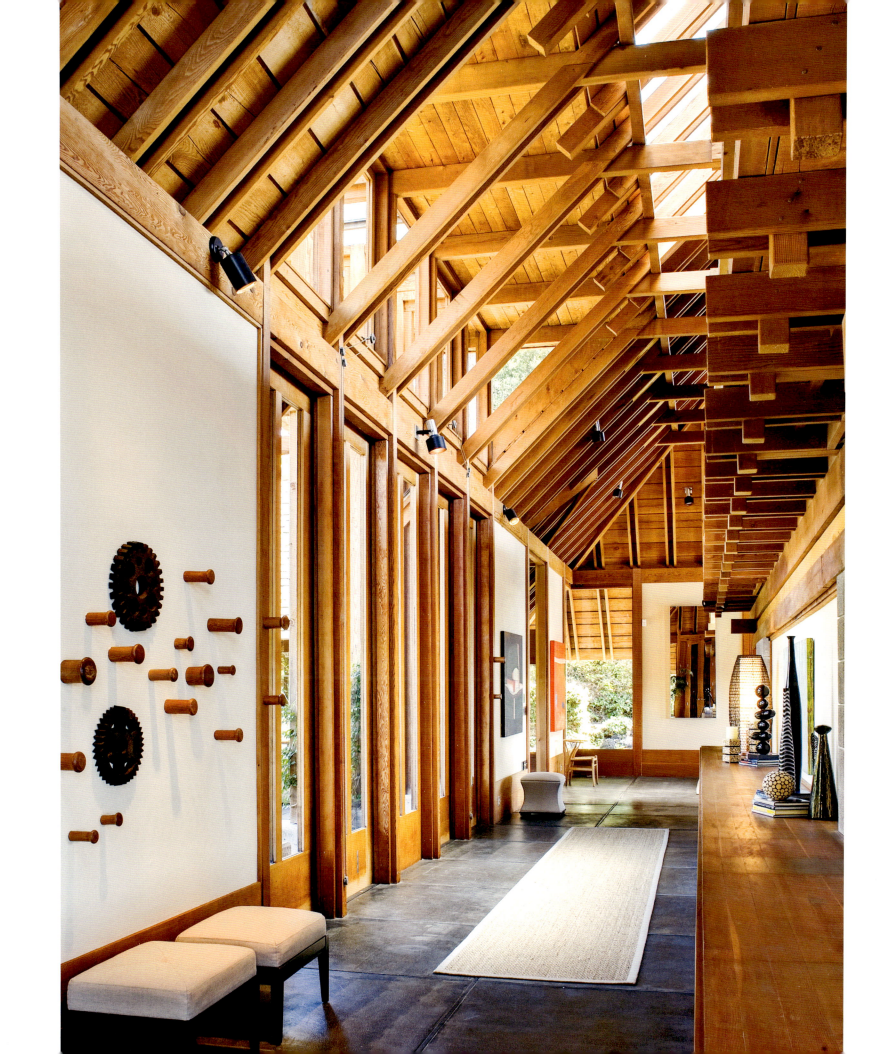

This spread Pool and entry into house, pool view to auto entry to north.

SOUVERAIN WINERY

RUTHERFORD, CALIFORNIA | 1971

Fred Holmes, owner of Souverain Winery, was introduced to Davis by Bud Mueller, Holmes's attorney and an investor in the winery. At Souverain, Davis took themes from his residential work and explored them at the much larger scale of a quasi-industrial complex. It is interesting to speculate on the influence of large agricultural barns that Davis undoubtedly saw growing up in Oklahoma.

At first glance, Souverain Winery is unmistakably a large barn. In a Napa Valley Register article, Davis recounted that the barn design "was used to make it relate with the county's past history." Like other Davis designs, the power of the single unifying roof form is present. Upon closer inspection though, the almost archetypal form reveals itself to be more complicated. The barn is nestled into the hillside, while the roof both floats above the ground and is tied to it by a structure of buttresses on the west flank. These buttresses seem to be resisting the thrust of the earth on the uphill side of the building. The roof is not a simple Gambrel but a series of layered planes.

Between the buttresses the roof plane is extended above a side passage by a trellis, which dematerializes the roof and accentuates it at the same time. Visitor reception and tasting areas, with offices above, inhabit the north end of the building, while winemaking functions occupy the balance. Four small gabled dormers add richness by accentuating the shift in roof slope and aligning with service doors below. Ridge vents included in the same location were eliminated in the final design, giving greater drama to the length of the building.

Above Davis later designed a grand landscape entry portal for the winery's cave complex. **Opposite page** North elevation, entry into tasting and offices.

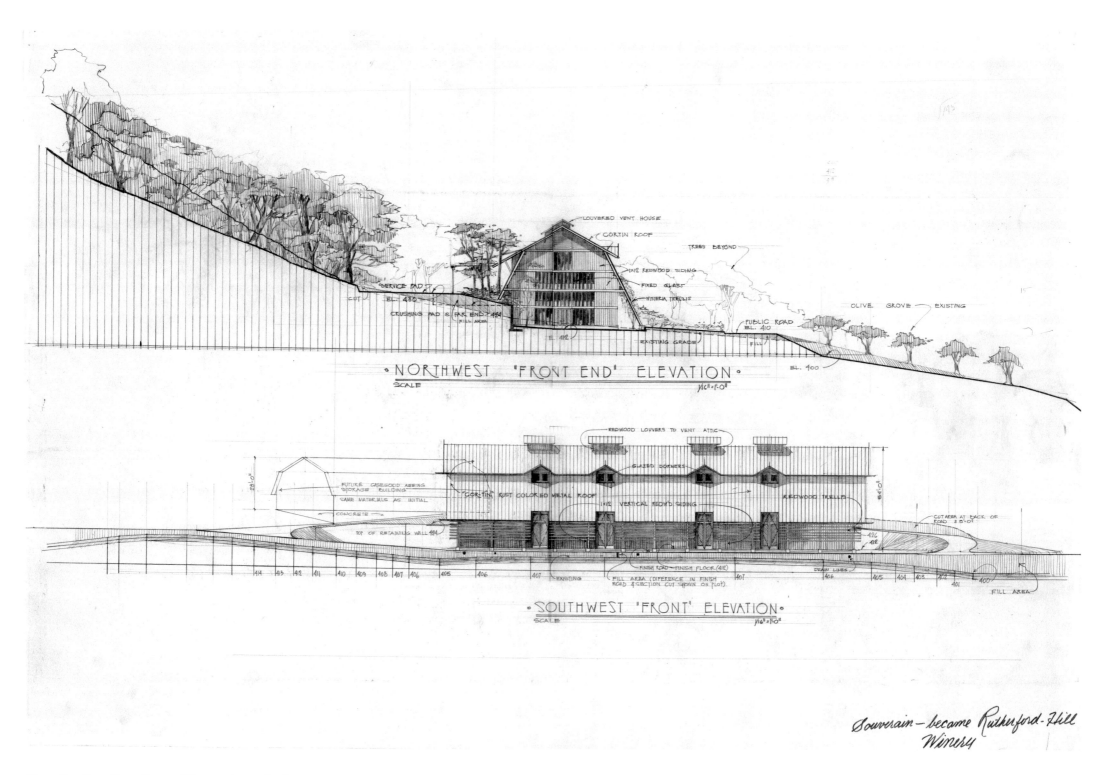

NORTHWEST "FRONT END" ELEVATION

SOUTHWEST "FRONT" ELEVATION

Souverain — became Rutherford-Hill Winery

Above Elevations. **Opposite page** Winery under construction.

"Upon closer inspection though, the almost archetypal form reveals itself to be more complicated."

—

Above left and right North elevation with grand entry doors. **Bottom left and Opposite page** Western elevation showing trellised extension of roof. **Bottom right** Roof detail.

CHATEAU SOUVERAIN

GEYSERVILLE, CALIFORNIA | 1972 (Substantially remodeled)

Chateau Souverain represented the Souverain Winery's foray into Sonoma County wines. Davis faced an even more complex challenge in terms of creating an architectural solution to an industrial facility.

The bulk of the winery is in fact a simple concrete building. Davis created a dramatic courtyard entry facing north. At each end of the short arms of the building are tower elements. These towers were modeled on old hop kilns found nearby on the Russian River. This form allowed Davis to use his signature powerful roof form on a building element that was small enough to be expressed. Strong eyebrow dormers connected the lower walls to the roof above, while the interior of each of these towers contained dramatic rooms that opened to the cupola above.

Davis designed a massive light fixture which hung in the east tower. Gabled roof elements connected the towers to the production building, a mansard roof with eyebrow dormers on the building created the courtyard space, providing an iconic image for the building.

The winery was purchased by Francis Ford Coppola for his Coppola Winery in 2005 and was remodeled.

Above Elevation. **Opposite page** Rendering by Violeta Autumn.

"Davis created a dramatic courtyard entry facing north. At each end of the short arms of the building are tower elements. These towers were modeled on old hop kilns found nearby on the Russian River."

—

Left John Marsh Davis and Barbara Davis Moore at Chateau Souverain. **Above** Hanging light designed by John Marsh Davis. **Opposite page** Chateau Souverain awning system.

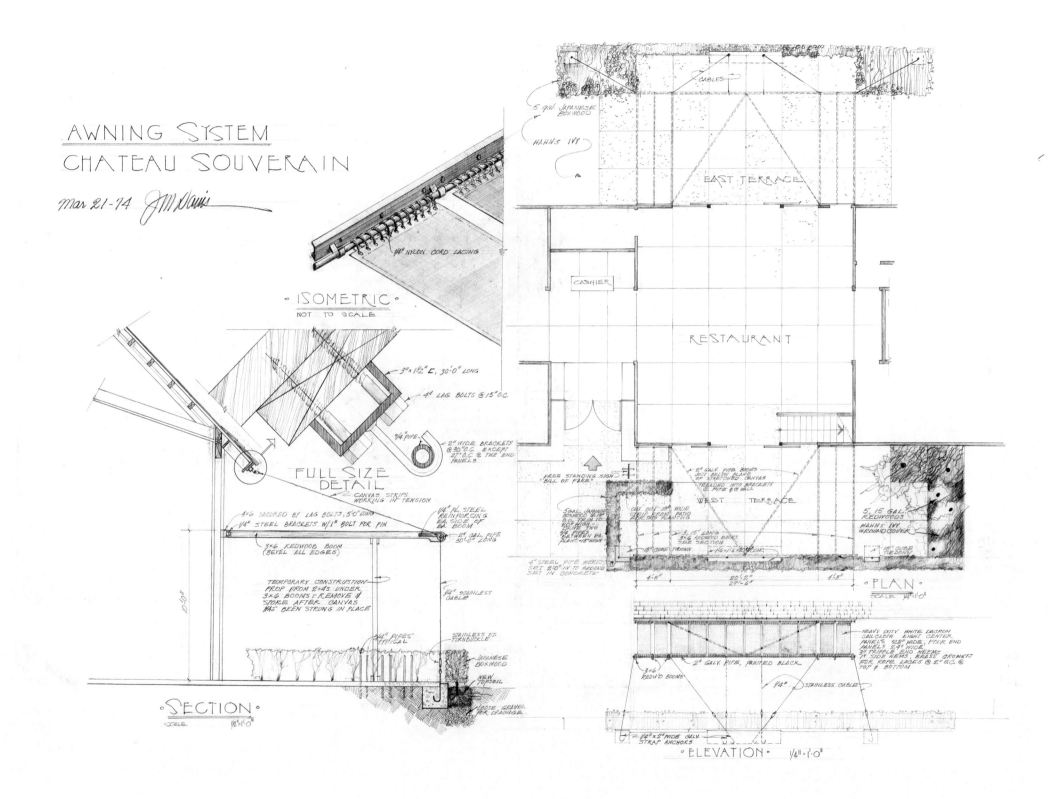

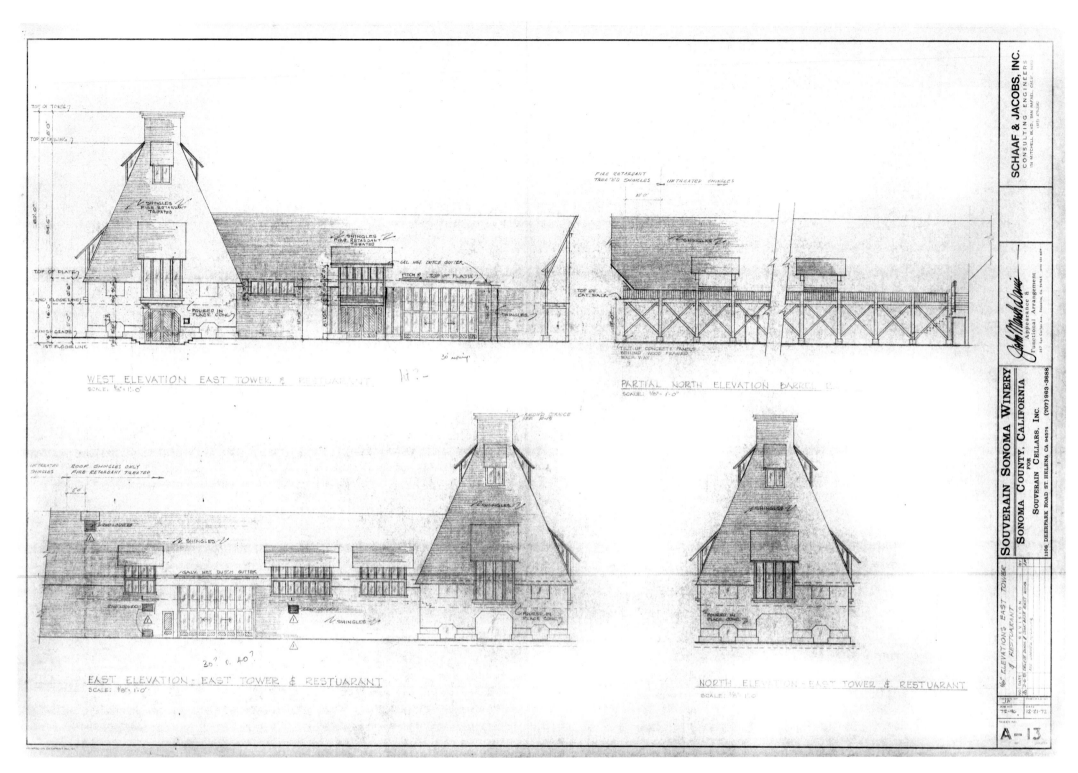

Above Elevations. **Opposite page** View of Northeast tower.

STONEBRIDGE WINERY V. 1

ST. HELENA, CALIFORNIA | 1972 (UNBUILT)

Joseph Phelps was a successful Colorado contractor who had a passion for wine. In the late 1960's, Phelps was simultaneously running one of the largest construction companies in the U.S., Hensel Phelps Construction, and beginning to make wine for himself, when he won the bid to build Souverain Winery (now Rutherford Hill) located a few miles outside St. Helena. It was through this connection, facilitated by Bud Mueller, that Joe met John Marsh Davis. The first property that Phelps purchased was on the southwest corner of Zinfandel Lane and the Silverado Trail, where a stone bridge crosses over the Napa River on the north side of the site.

Stonebridge was the name for the proposed winery that Joe Phelps asked Davis to design. The first scheme is an interesting evolution of elements from the Rutherford Hill project, with a significant, character defining addition: a large bridge-like element at the top ridge of the roof, projecting out over the entry like the prow of a ship and aligned with the historic stone bridge.

The production facility is articulated as a stone building with large wood doors covered by a Gambrel roof – a version of Souverain Rutherford. The roof is less barn like – with its shallow slope it provides the counterpoint to the dramatic rooftop ridge/bridge which was to house tasting rooms and offices. This bridge would end up being realized in a different form in the Joseph Phelps winery as it was ultimately built.

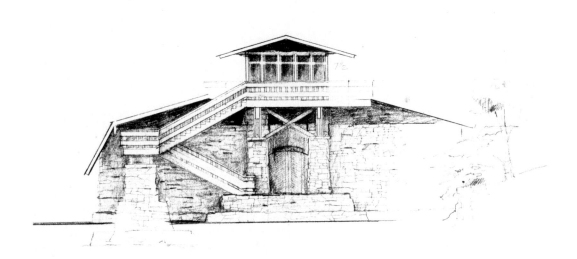

Above West elevation variant with stair. **Opposite page** Davis' rendering of the first stonebridge winery scheme.

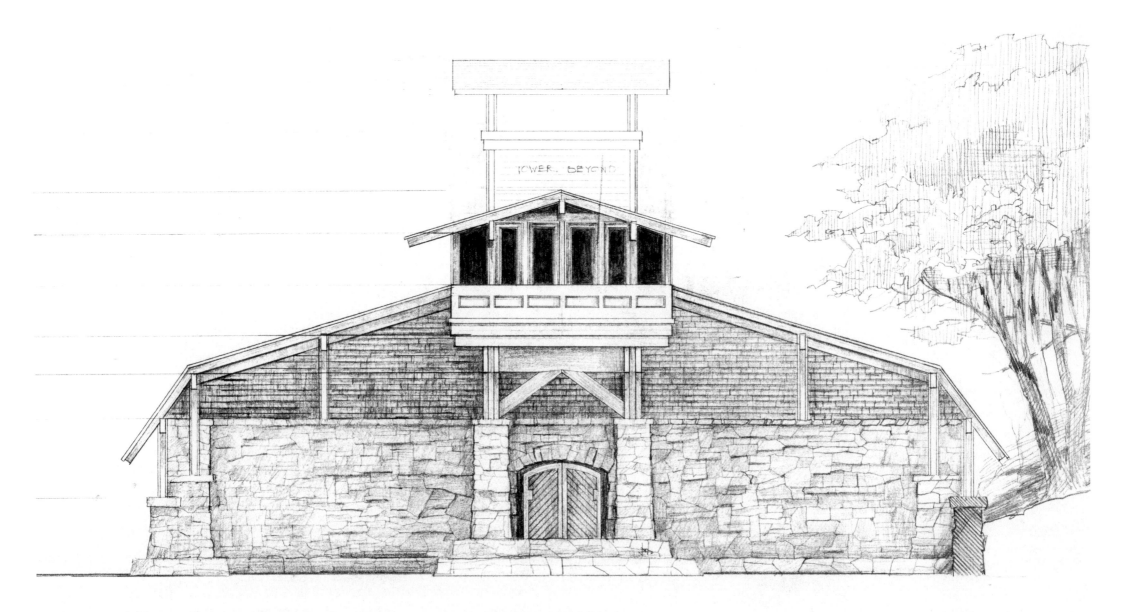

IE WEST ELEVATION "END" AS SEEN FROM THE STONE BRIDGE ON ZINFANDEL LANE

Above West elevation. **Opposite page** North elevation and plan.

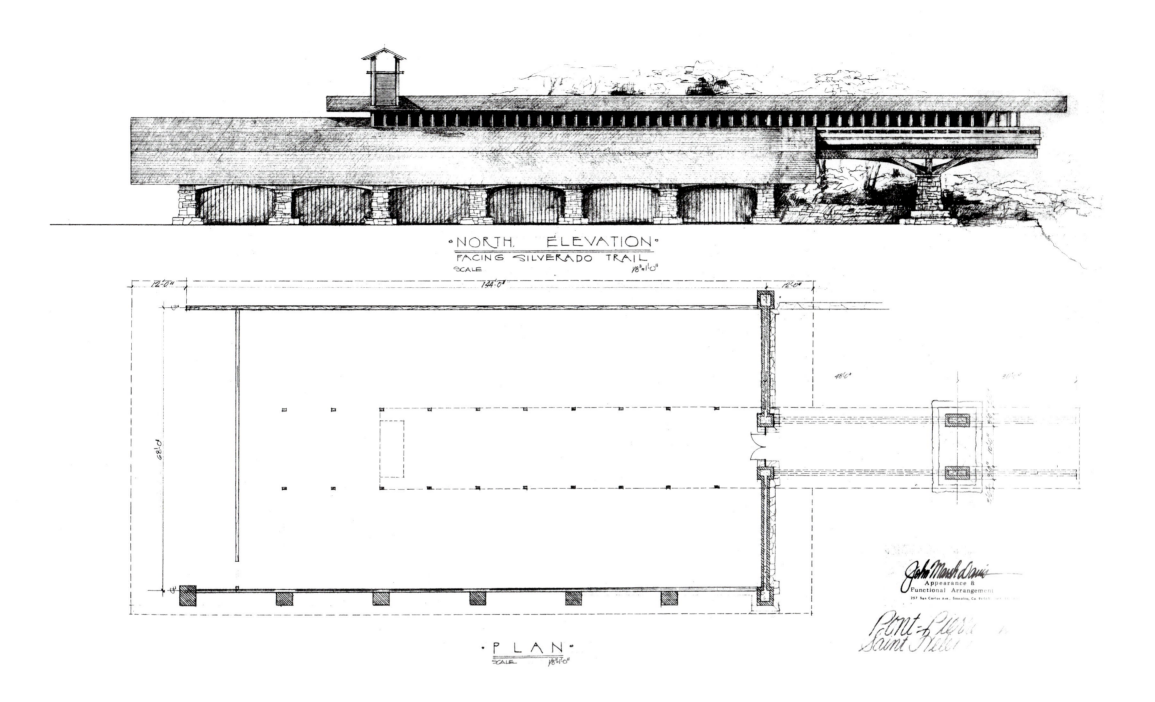

·NORTH· ELEVATION·
FACING SILVERADO TRAIL
SCALE 1/8"=1'-0"

· P L A N ·
SCALE 1/8"=1'-0"

John Marsh Davis
Appearance &
Functional Arrangement

"The first scheme is an interesting evolution of elements from the Rutherford Hill project, with a significant, character defining addition: a large bridge-like element at the top ridge of the roof, projecting out over the entry like the prow of a ship and aligned with the historic stone bridge."

STONEBRIDGE WINERY V. 2

ST. HELENA, CALIFORNIA | 1972 (UNBUILT)

Subsequent to developing the masonry scheme, Davis produced a design of a wood structure for the Stonebridge site based around a courtyard. This scheme is clearly for the flat site along the Silverado Trail, but it has many elements that would ultimately find their way into the Joseph Phelps Winery.

The basic parti has two main wings, each with a head building mass that is linked by a bridge. In this way, the bridge of the first Stonebridge scheme is given real meaning as a connecting element, and creates a gateway into a landscaped courtyard.

Davis was very interested in landscape, and toward the end of his career would devote a substantial amount of his time to both landscape design and gardening. Here he introduces an ideal garden into the heart of his design.

The single elevation for the project shows Davis's trademark layering of roof forms both as roofs and dormer roofs. The bridge form is an exploration of bracketed wood construction.

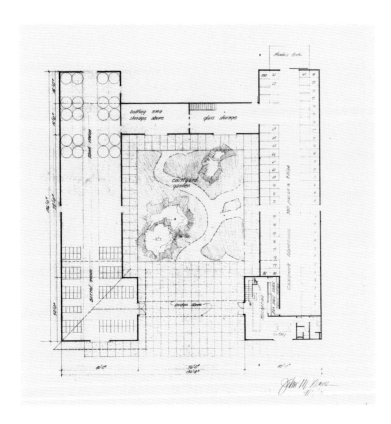

Above Ground floor plan. **Opposite page** West elevation showing courtyard beyond bridge.

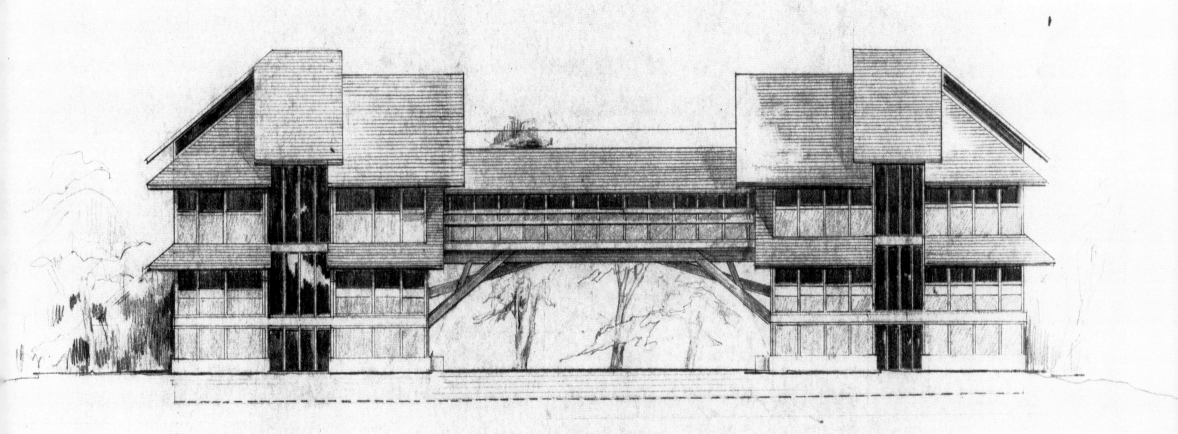

·WEST ELEVATION – COURTYARD BEYOND BRIDGE SPAN·

SCALE   ⅛"=1'-0"

JOSEPH PHELPS VINEYARDS

ST. HELENA, CALIFORNIA | 1973

Joseph Phelps acquired the Spring Valley Ranch to the northeast of the Stonebridge site and decided that it was here that he would build his winery and later his home.

Davis' basic concept for the winery seems to have evolved quickly and the first drawings we have are close to the executed project. The parti is in many respects a synthesis of the prior schemes for a dramatically different site. Phelps decided that he wanted a winery that would reveal itself to the visitor after a procession up onto a ridge overlooking the small valley. One comes upon the east side of the facility – a pair of barns linked by a bridge – almost by surprise after having driven around them.

A 120' trellis extends from the hillside through the break between the two barns, inviting visitors into the complex and suggesting that they continue west to the view side of the property. Here the idealized garden is replaced by the ideal of nature. Redwood forest on the hill above gives way to the mighty oaks overlooking the valley that is the heart of Joseph Phelps Vineyards. Originally the North Building was the wine production and the South barrel aging. The North Building had a small sales shop and access to the two upper levels – one in the building itself and the other in the bridge level. A similar stair came down and through the South Building. The stair rise and run echoes the roof slope which establishes the geometry of the diagonal paneling used throughout. This geometry is also found in the diagonals of the great entry truss.

Above Western terrace with repurposed John Marsh Davis trellis, looking out over the vineyard. **Opposite page** Entry.

The exterior of the building is sheathed in Redwood board and batten. In fact, the winery is an ingenious mixture of Redwood and Douglas Fir – where most of the structural members (except the trellises) are Fir and paneling is Redwood. Custom-made doors that feature diagonal infill are Fir with Redwood accent trim. Joe Phelps tells of using salvaged virgin Redwood for the project that he obtained while building a new highway bridge in Sonoma County. The hipped ends to the barn roofs pull the composition together as one sees the two buildings as halves of a complete whole. The paneling in the entry – which was composed of 1x6 boards with projecting 1xtrim with plywood panels – is characteristic of his work at the time.

Like his other winery projects, the working drawings were done by Keith & Associates and his client in this case was the contractor. Phelps tells of having set up a special shop onsite to custom build all the doors and windows. Bill Phelps, Joe's son and current Executive Chairman of the winery, worked on the construction crew. Joe Phelps added to and modified the winery over the years, including projects he did on his own – the oval room and expansion of the North Building and, with Davis, the new sales room and tasting facility in the South Building. This project, designed in 1989, reflects the later period of Davis's work. It is more refined in its use of highly finished redwood paneling, which reveals his ongoing fascination with the work of the Greene brothers.

Above Cross section through the central opening and offices. **Opposite page** Preliminary entry elevation and Site landscape plan.

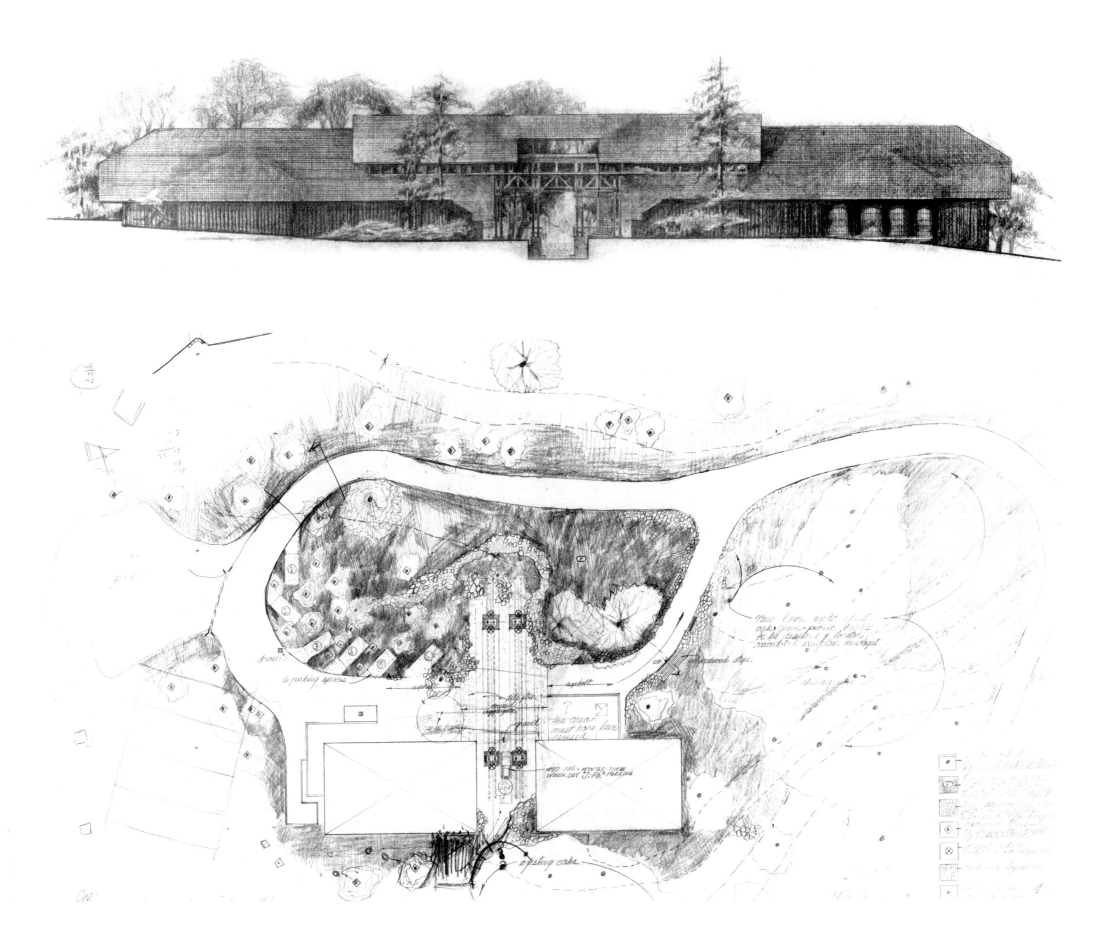

Above Joe Phelps and assistant winemaker Bruce Rogers on the construction site. **Below right** Photo of Bill Phelps on the winery construction site. **Below left** Joe Phelps with winemaker Walter Schug reviewing drawings of the winery, Joseph Phelps Vineyards under construction in the background. **Opposite page** Aerial view at the time of construction.

Wine production eventually moved into a facility closer to Silverado Trail. The Phelps family commissioned BCV Architecture + Interiors and Don Brandenburger, AIA, to renovate the building, including converting the North Building into a large visitors center. A new path leads guests from the parking area through the Redwood island to the east of the Great Trellis, where a stair takes them on axis through to the entry, thus heightening the original arrival experience. The interior reception rooms explore the difference between the east and west sides of the building – a theme central to Davis's work. At the heart of the visitor center is a great gallery hall defined by trusses.

Above East elevation showing new tasting rooms and offices. **Opposite page** New entry path to trellis.

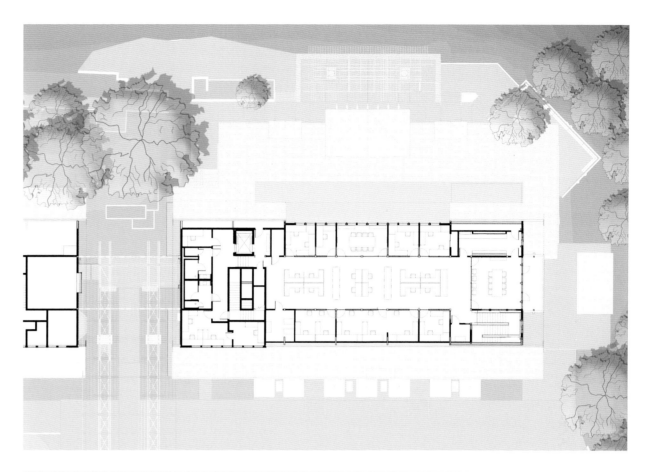

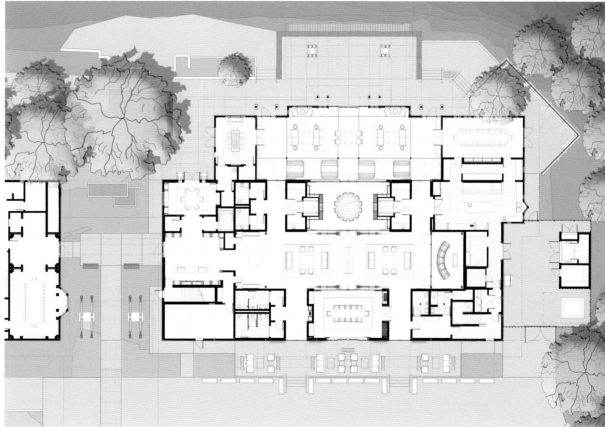

Opposite page Site plan of Joseph Phelps Vineyards. Drawing by BCV Architecture + Interiors. **Right top** Second floor office plan showing offices above. **Right bottom** Main floor plan of new visitor center in old winery production building.

This spread New entry path to trellis.

Opposite page above Bacchus tasting room. **Opposite page bottom** Reception area with original light fixture designed by Davis. **Above** Great Hall.

Above Wine library looking to barrel room. **Opposite page** Views of Joseph Phelps Vineyards visitor center and new offices.

Above Barrel room. **Opposite page bottom left** New stair to second floor offices. **Opposite page bottom right** Insignia tasting room. **Opposite page top** Western terrace with repurposed John Marsh Davis trellis.

"The stair rise and run echoes the roof slope which establishes the geometry of the diagonal paneling used throughout. This geometry is also found in the diagonals of the great entry truss."

—

Above New west entry to oval room. **Below and opposite** Western terrace with repurposed John Marsh Davis trellis. **Next spread** Western elevation taken from vineyards.

SULLIVAN VINEYARDS

RUTHERFORD, CALIFORNIA | 1974

Jim Sullivan was a successful graphic artist, known for his work with legendary 60s groups like The Monkees and Dick Clark Productions. Jim and his wife, JoAnna, purchased the property that would become Sullivan Vineyards in 1972, as he had been nurturing an interest in growing and making wine.

Located in Rutherford off Galleron Road, in the heart of Napa Valley, the site had been carefully chosen by Jim through extensive studies into local terroir. The Sullivan's concept of terroir had three requirements: location, dry farming and winemaking style. The area, known as the Rutherford Bench, featured a water table 6-10' deep with sandy loam soils.

James Halliday, writing in "The Wine Atlas of California," notes that John Marsh Davis, "...designed an inspired house which makes you feel you are on a hilltop cathedral, rather than the flat valley floor: it literally floats in space." Davis' signature wood detailing is apparent in the house, particularly at the skylight at the top of the central stair that connects each level. On the second floor, an expansive deck off one of the function rooms overlooks the surrounding vineyards, with large sliding doors that open the interior to the north and west.

The site plan was organized based on the cardinal directions as Davis' drawing of the site make explicit.

The winemaking barn and the house were intended to be knit together by bridges, which were never realized. The courtyard was designed to accomodate the turning radius of a car and the buildings integrate the arrival by car into their design -- which is characteristc of many of Davis' projects. The galley kitchen in the house is one of the most generous of Davis' kitchens.

Above Early study through courtyard looking north to house. Note: deck extensions. **Opposite page** House porte-cochère.

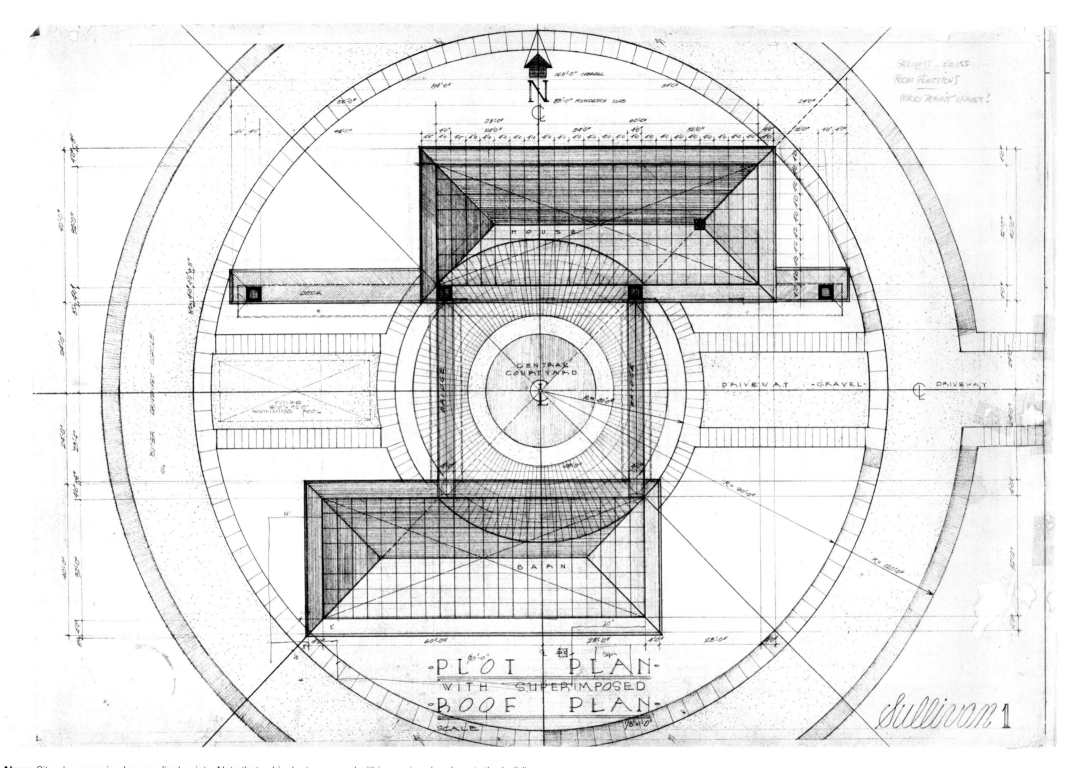

Above Site plan organized on cardinal points. Note that vehicular turnaround within courtyard undercuts the buildings.

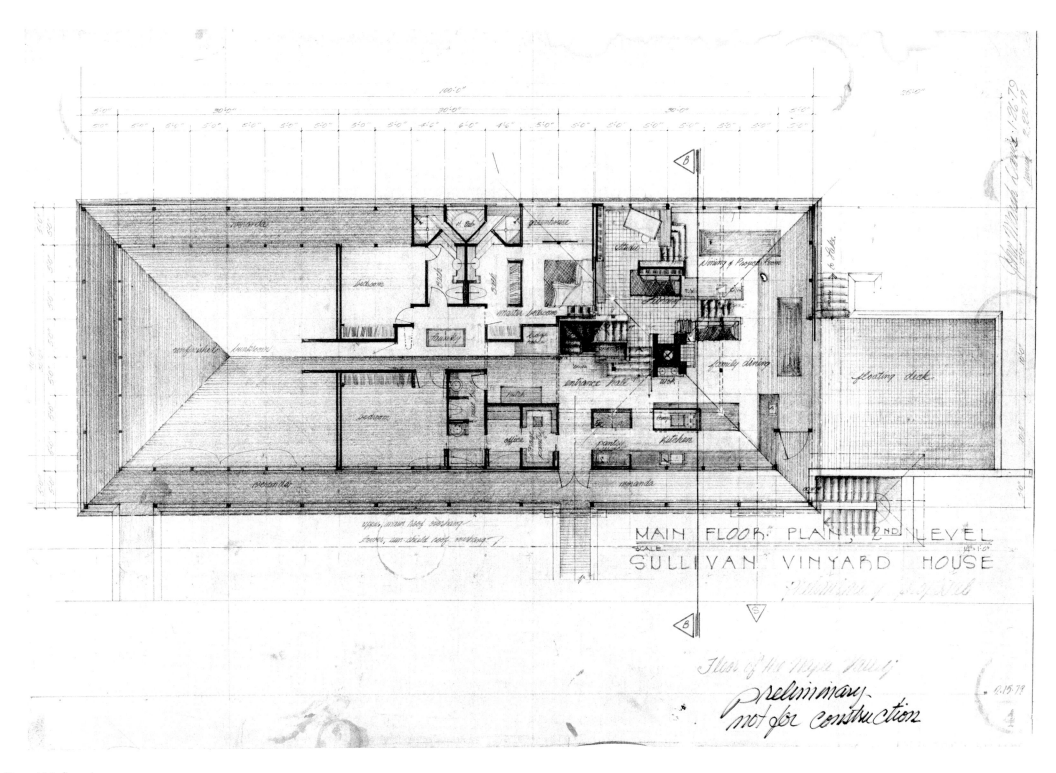

MAIN FLOOR PLAN, 2ND LEVEL
SULLIVAN VINYARD HOUSE

preliminary
not for construction

Above Main floor plan.

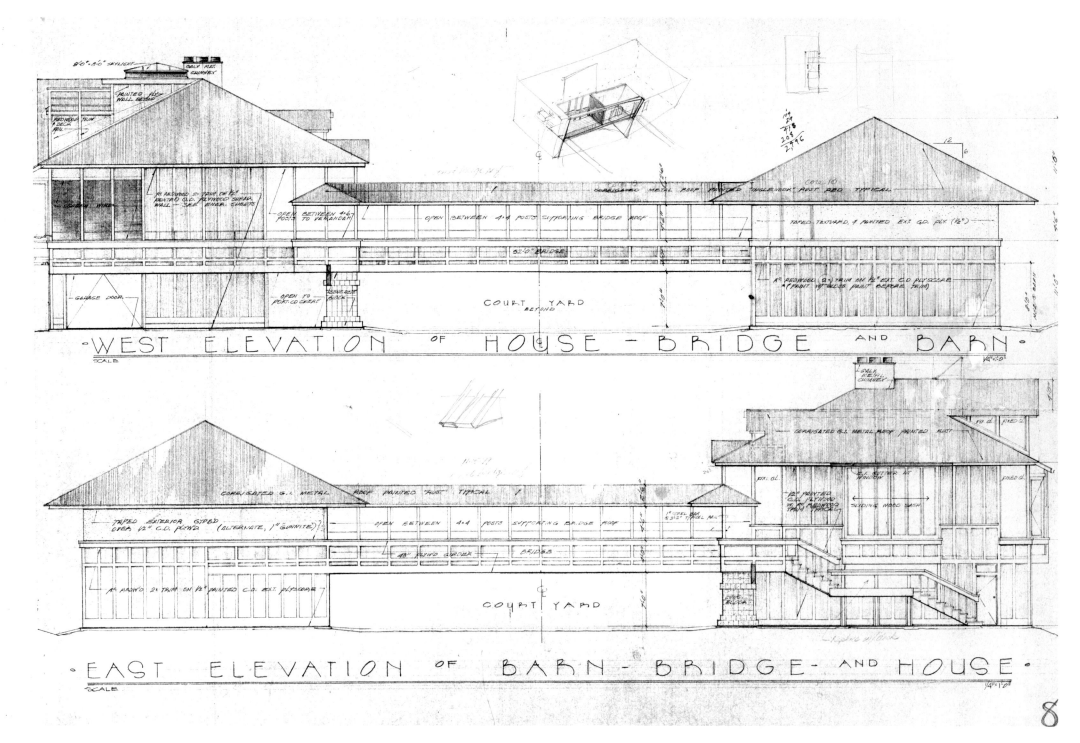

Above East and west elevations of house and barn showing unbuilt connecting bridge. **Opposite page** North and south house elevation; North and south barn elevation.

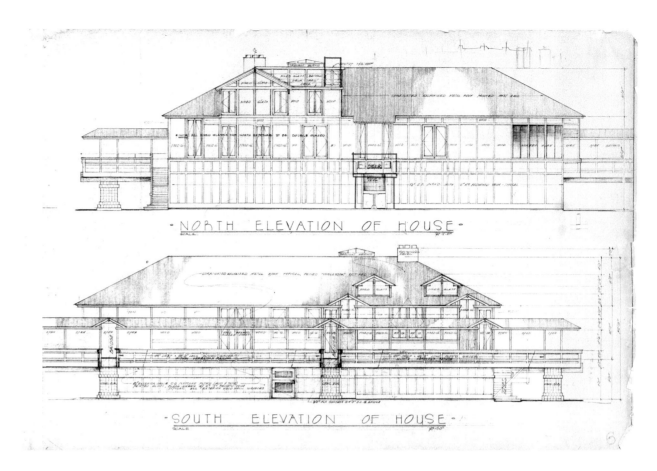

·NORTH ELEVATION OF HOUSE·

·SOUTH ELEVATION OF HOUSE·

6

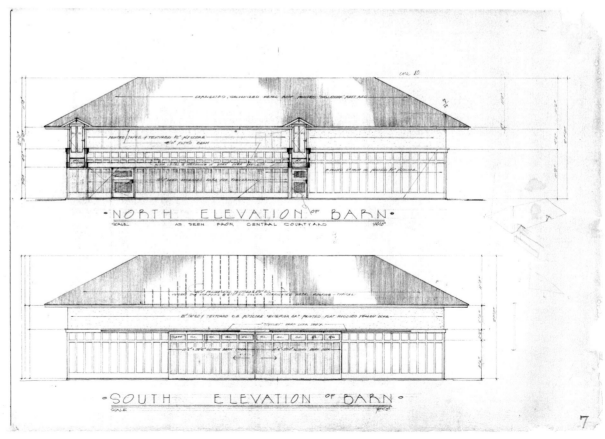

·NORTH ELEVATION OF BARN·

·SOUTH ELEVATION OF BARN·

7

Opposite page View of stairwell from Northwest with chimney mass beyond. **Above** Winery barn room showing infilled porte-cochère. **Bottom** Entry.

" The courtyard was designed to accomodate the turning radius of a car and the buildings integrate the arrival by car into their design – which is characteristc of many of Davis' projects. The galley kitchen in the house is one of the most generous of Davis' kitchens. "

—

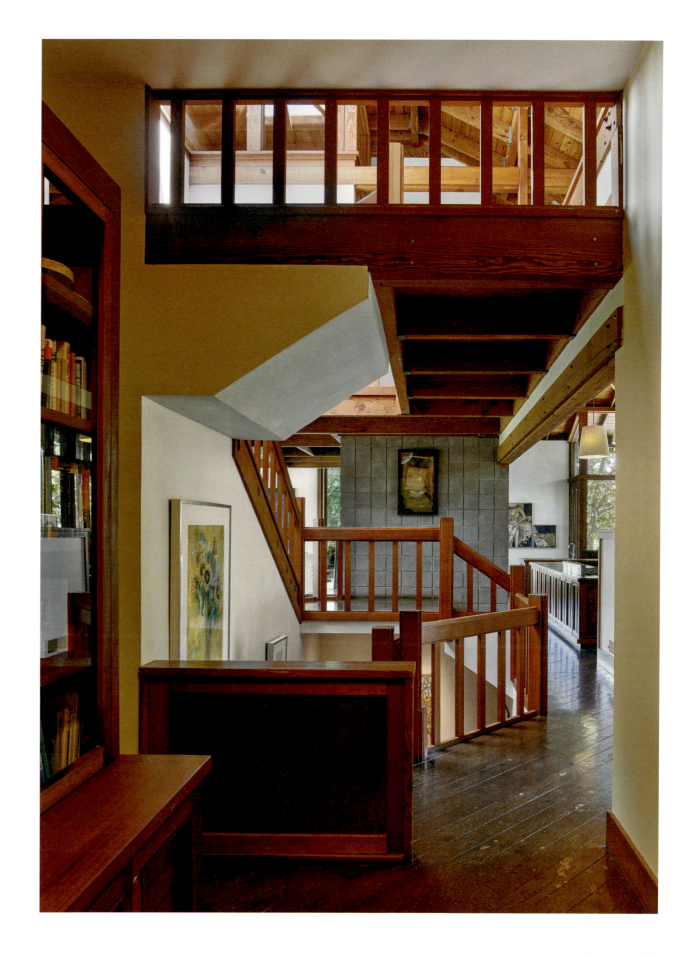

Above Main house kitchen and dining room fireplace. **Opposite page** View of dining room fireplace and kitchen.

Above Northwest corner room opens onto the deck. **Opposite page** North elevation.

THACHER RESIDENCE

SONOMA, CALIFORNIA | 1974

Jim and Mary Thacher hired John Marsh Davis in 1974 to design a home for their family on Bald Mountain. They were moving their young family from San Francisco and lived on site throughout the construction of the house. David Thacher remembers that while the house costs exceeded any budget his parents had contemplated, they bought fully into Davis' vision. The house is a tour de force — sitting not on the top of the hill, but off to the side. Visitors enter the main floor where all the public rooms are located — looking out across to the south view. Two great sliding doors lead to a deck, that, when open, dissolve the line between interior and exterior. An upper pavilion roof structure houses the main rooms. Distinctly, it is rotated 45 degrees off the geometry of the lower level of the house, which is essentially a concrete structure dug into the side of the hill.

The wooden structure of the house is dominated by a giant truss that allows the great column free space of the house.

The great south facing deck originally was designed to have dramatic overlooks that extended on the two ends — these proved to be structurally unfeasible. The dining and living rooms are defined by the two great fireplaces. Small powder rooms (above the bathrooms below) are accessed by small decks sitting off the dining and living rooms, respectively. The kitchen and its table are located in the notch of the "L" directly opposite the sliding doors.

The Thacher residence is one of Davis' most inventive designs. He works to dematerialize the house through the act of rotating the roof structure, thus allowing it to shelter both interior and exterior space.

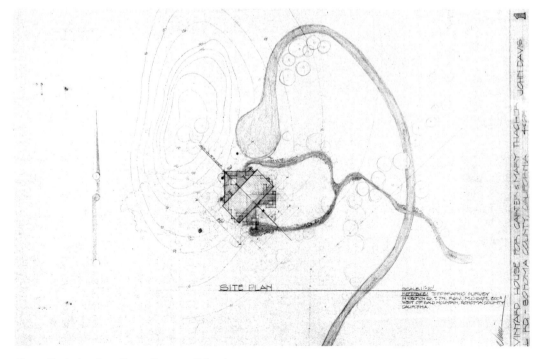

Above East elevation. **Opposite page** Entry view.

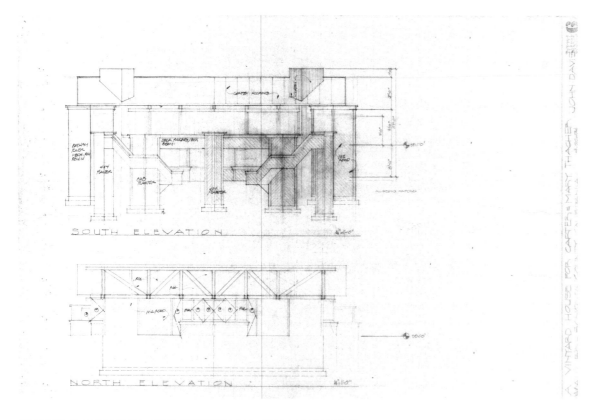

Above South and north elevations. **Bottom** East elevation and stair details.

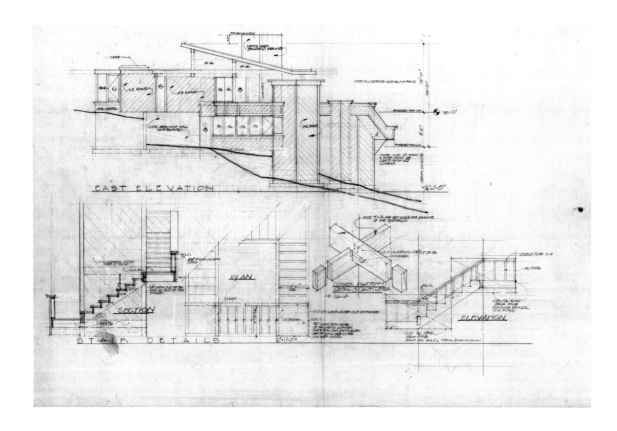

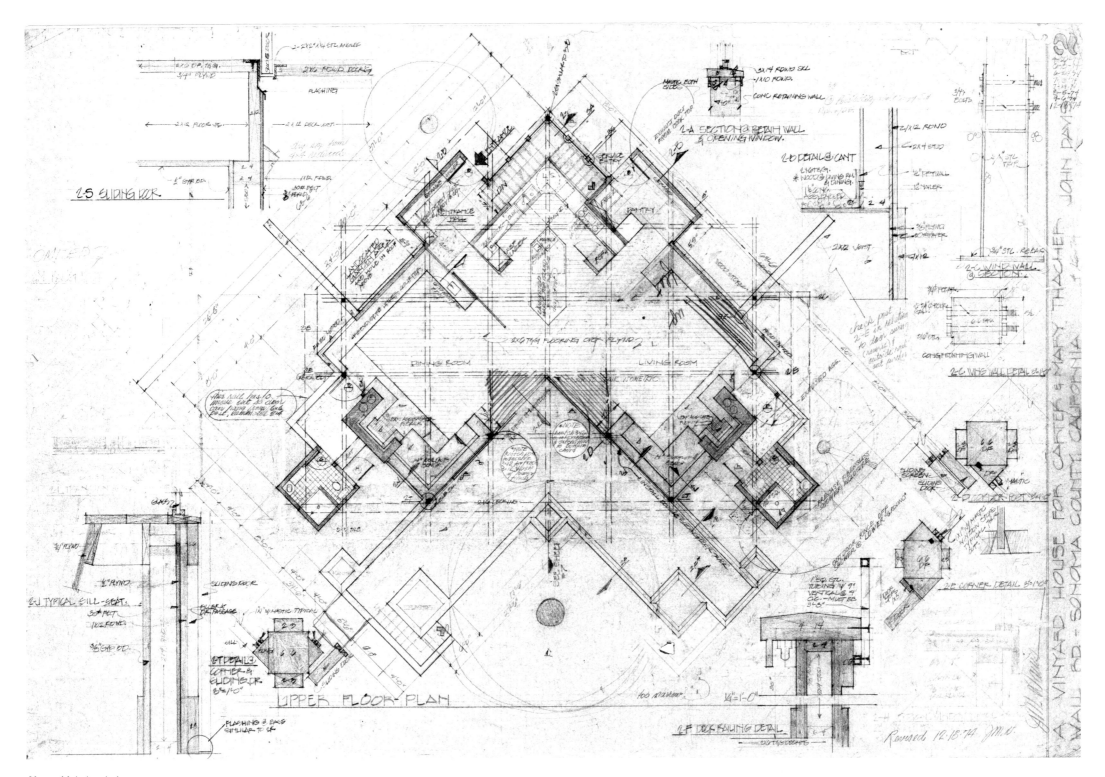

Above Main level plan.

Above Model exploring the geometries of the hoiuse. **Bottom** John Marsh Davis with the Thachers. **Opposite page** Thacher children watching construction. Construction view from west. Foundation form work, construction photo from Southwest. Pouring foundation wall.

Opposite page View from northwest. **Above** Layered roof form.

Left Great trussed roof over living room (foreground) extending to dining room beyond. **Opposite page** Living room.

" The Thacher residence is one of Davis' most inventive designs. He works to dematerialize the house through the act of rotating the roof structure, thus allowing it to shelter both interior and exterior space. "

—

Opposite page Kitchen island with dining room beyond **Right** Dining room and its fireplace on east side of house.

Above and bottom The south west deck. **Opposite page** The southwest deck with sliding doors into living room.

Above Entry - the symmetrical entry to the east leads to the kitchen pantry, the kitchen at center overlooks the stairs down to the bedroom. Main entry to right. **Opposite page** Kitchen. **Next spread** View of Thacher residence from the south.

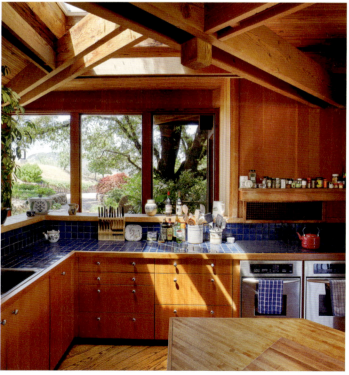

96 SANTA ROSA RESIDENCE

SAUSALITO, CALIFORNIA | 1978

John Marsh Davis designed 96 Santa Rosa in Sausalito for himself. In this project he compressed a rich variety of overlapping spaces that he visually extended throughout his signature use of mirrors. Like his earlier designs, the fireplace hearth creates a focus for the living room and partitions are treated as pieces of furniture to allow the larger space to be perceived or through mirrors reflected back.

This project looks forward to Davis' projects of the 80's and 90's, which were more refined in their detailing. Gone are the open joist ceilings and the overt expression of structure – replaced by a more finished and crafted approach.

The Phoenix Leasing building that was completed the following year represents the culmination of Davis' "Wood Expressionist" phase as the lessons of 96 Santa Rosa came to be applied more and more. Many of Davis' spatial interests remained the same – the dramatization of the hearth and the sheltering roof. But the projects are insistent in a new way – perhaps more sophisticated, but less elemental, less reductive.

Above Site plan. **Opposite page** View of living room with fireplace and a mirror which doubles window wall, Published in House Beautiful Magazine (1984)

" This project looks forward to Davis' projects of the 80's and 90's, which were more refined in their detailing. "

—

Opposite page View of living room, Published in House Beautiful Magazine (1984). **Above** Floor plan.

PHOENIX LEASING BUILDING

MILL VALLEY, CALIFORNIA | 1979

The Phoenix Leasing Building occupies a site on the north side of Miller Avenue in Mill Valley. Completed in 1979, Davis identifies this project as his favorite building in his personal photo albums. What he meant by this notation can never be fully known, but it clearly suggests that he felt he had achieved something special.

The building is placed at an angle on its site to improve solar orientation and create a larger private yard on the west side (rear) of the building and more parking close to the street. The building is a singular shape composed of a complex double-layered truss in section that extends both inside and outside the enclosing walls. The east side of the building is at a higher elevation than the west, and one enters into a long gallery which provides symmetrical sets of stairs up to a bridge that leads up or a set of stairs that leads down to the main floor. The open workspace on this western ground floor is defined by its massive sets of double doors, which are 15 feet tall.

On the east side each bay has a projecting wisteria laden trellis. The trellis structure extends from inside to outside and the extensive use of glass further reinforces the sense of transparency in this building. Structure and architecture are one in the same. The roof transforms into wall and the levels interweave spatially. Circulation weaves throughout the structure. As with so many of Davis's buildings of the period, it is clear that he is interested in how the eastern entry side of the building is different from the western view side. Here he designed special canvas awnings to protect from the harsh afternoon sun. The east was designed to be appreciated from the exterior, the west more from the interior.

The working drawings for this project recognize that Violeta Eidelman Autumn (1930-2012) was working with Davis. She was one of the first women to receive a bachelor of architecture degree from the University of Oklahoma.

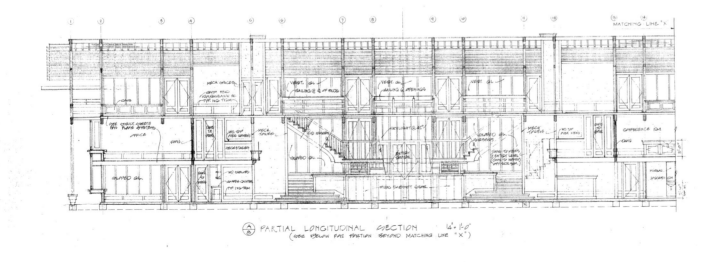

Above Section. Opposite page South Elevation.

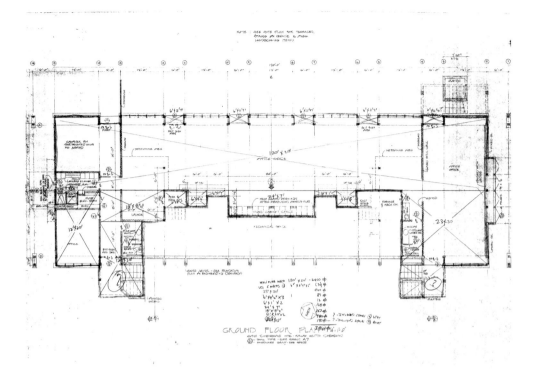

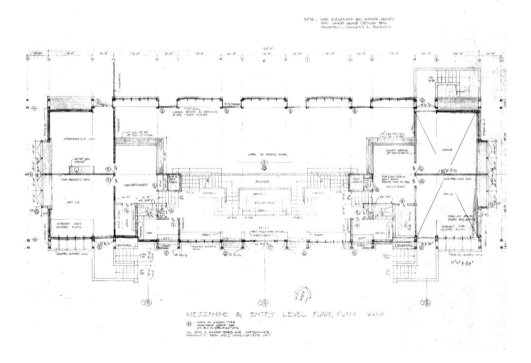

Above Mezzanine & entry level floor plan.

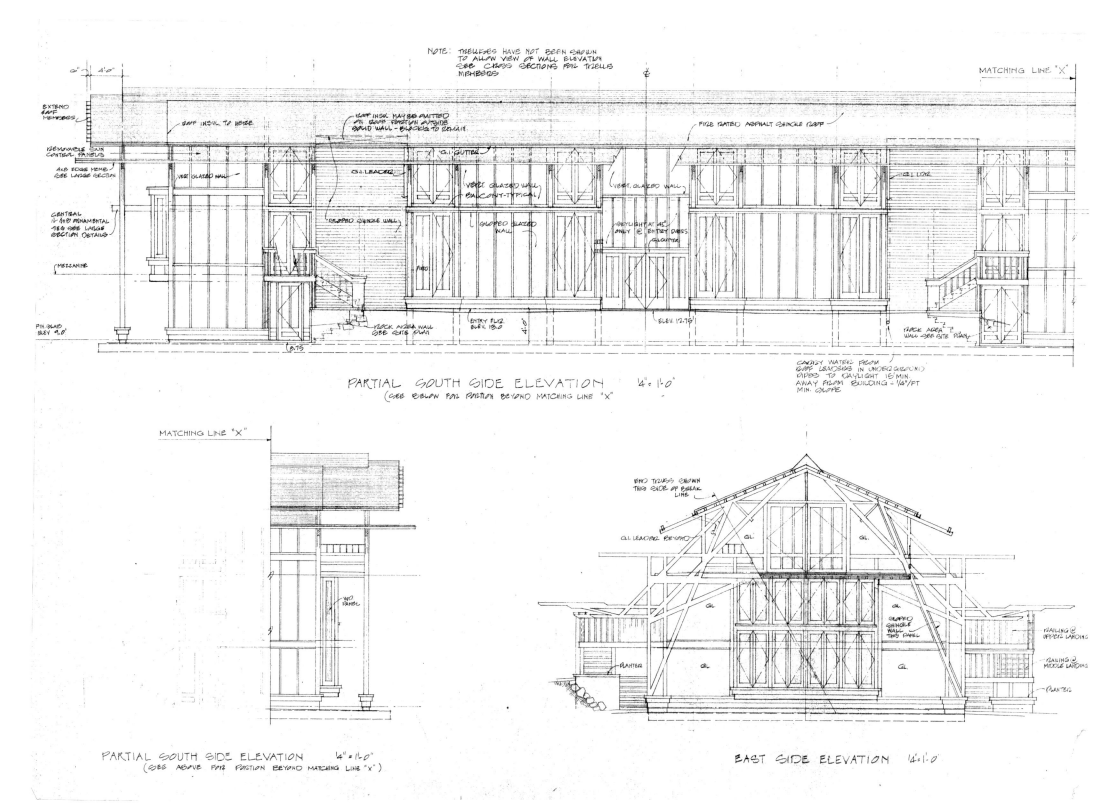

NOTE: TRELLISES HAVE NOT BEEN SHOWN TO ALLOW VIEW OF WALL ELEVATION. SEE CROSS SECTIONS FOR TRELLIS MEMBERS

MATCHING LINE "X"

EXTEND ROOF MEMBERS

ROOF INSUL. TO REMAIN

ROOF INSUL. MAY BE OMITTED ON ROOF PORTION OUTSIDE SOLID WALL - BLOCKS TO REMAIN

FIRE RATED ASPHALT SHINGLE ROOF

REMOVABLE SUN CONTROL PANELS

4X8 EDGE MEMB SEE LARGE SECTION

G.I. GUTTER

VERT GLAZED WALL

G.I. LEADER

CENTRAL 4X8 ORNAMENTAL TIES SEE LARGE SECTION DETAILS

VERT. GLAZED WALL

VERT GLAZED WALL BALCONY-TYPICAL

GLAZED SHINGLE WALL

GLAZED GLAZED WALL

G.I. LDR

SKYLIGHT AT 45° ONLY @ ENTRY DOORS

MEZZANINE

G.I. GUTTER

FIN GRADE ELEV 9.0

ROCK AREA WALL SEE SITE PLAN

ENTRY FLR. ELEV. 13.0

ELEV. 12.75

ROCK AREA WALL SEE SITE PLAN

9.75

CANOPY WATER FROM ROOF LEADERS IN UNDERGROUND PIPES TO DAYLIGHT 16' MIN AWAY FROM BUILDING - 1/4"/FT MIN. SLOPE

PARTIAL SOUTH SIDE ELEVATION   1/4" = 1'-0"
(SEE BELOW FOR PORTION BEYOND MATCHING LINE "X")

MATCHING LINE "X"

WD PANEL

PARTIAL SOUTH SIDE ELEVATION   1/4" = 1'-0"
(SEE ABOVE FOR PORTION BEYOND MATCHING LINE "X")

END TRUSS SHOWN THIS SIDE OF BREAK LINE

G.I. LEADER BEYOND

GL

GL

GL

GL

GLAZED SHINGLE WALL THIS PANEL

GL

GL

PLANTER

RAILING @ UPPER LANDING

RAILING @ MIDDLE LANDING

PLANTER

EAST SIDE ELEVATION   1/4" = 1'-0"

Above South side elevation and details.

"As with so many of Davis's buildings of the period, it is clear that he is interested in how the eastern entry side of the building is different from the western view side."

—

Left East entry.

Above Left Entry from the east. **Above Right** Main office space on the west with trusses weaving through the building. **Below** Cross-sections. **Opposite** Stair detail at eastern entry.

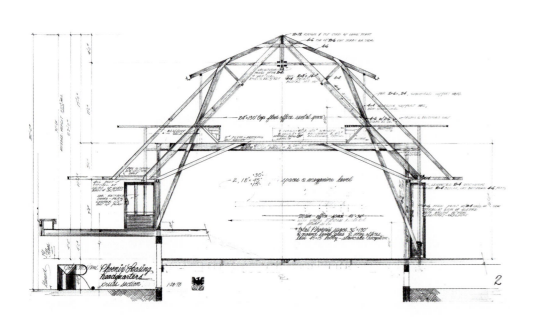

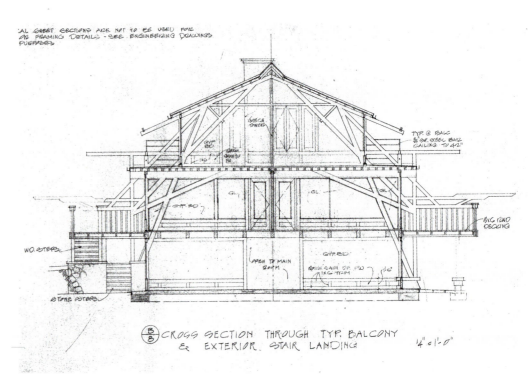

Above Entry. Below Rendering by Violeta Autumn of variant scheme from Southeast. Right View from southeast.

PHOENIX LEASING INC.

APPENDIX

PROJECT LIST

This list is based on drawings and fragmentary information, and is as complete as we could make it at the time of publication. It is intended to further future research into John Marsh Davis' projects.

1961 – Lampton Residence, Sapulpa, OK
1962 – Residence, 2 Harrison Avenue, Sausalito, CA
1962 – JM Davis Residence, 174 Harrison Avenue, Sausalito, CA
1962/1970 – JM Davis Residence, 101 San Carlos Avenue, Sausalito, CA
1963 – Fidangue Residence, Sausalito, CA
1963 – Residence, 199 Bulkley Avenue, Sausalito, CA
1965 – Donald Barbour Residence, 45 Vista Drive, Kentfield, CA
1965 – Adolf Mueller Residence, 455 Belvedere Avenue, Belvedere, CA
1965 – Druckerman-Liddell Residence, Mill Valley, CA
1966 – JM Davis Residence, 33 Calle del Sierra, Stinson Beach, CA
1966 – Eric Barnett Residence, 1599 S. Whitehall Lane, Helena, CA
1968 – Werdegar Residence
1968 – Alexander Imlay Residence, Sausalito, CA
1969 – Bill & Molly Sterling Residence, 625 Lovell Avenue, Mill Valley, CA
1969 – James Roush Residence, 2441 Evergreen Point Road, Medina, WA
1970 – Ted and Ruth Nash Residence, 16 Crest Road, Belvedere, CA
1971 – Souverain Winery, 200 Rutherford Road, Rutherford, CA
1972 – Chateau Souverain Winery, 400 Souverain Road, Geyserville, CA
1972 – Peter Ross Residence, 61 Upper Road, Ross, CA
1973 – Joseph Phelps Winery, 200 Taplin Road, St. Helena, CA
1974 – Sullivan Vineyards Winery, 1090 Galleron Road, Rutherford, CA
1974 – Carter & Mary Thacher Residence, 400 Wall Road, Sonoma, CA
1975 – Otis Guy Bacon Residence, 202 Woods Lane, Ardmore, OK
1978 – David Brown Residence, 602 Quincy Avenue, Long Beach, CA
1978 – Joan Mueller Remodel, 2431 Mar East Road, Belvedere, CA

ODIS SHOAF RESIDENCE
THE FOLIAGE - WICHITA, KANSAS

Odis Shoaf Residence, Wichita, KS. 1993.

Weissman Residence, Carmel, CA. 1983.

2

10·1

JULIAN·RIDGEFIELD

9·15·88

Julian Residence, Ridgefield, CT. 1992.

Trees Residence, San Francisco, CA. 1997.

1978 – JM Davis Residence, 96 Santa Rosa Avenue, Sausalito, CA
1979 – Phoenix Leasing Commercial, 495 Miller Ave, Mill Valley, CA
1981 – Residence, 61 Lee Street, Mill Valley, CA
1983 – Weissman Residence, 499 Aguajito Road, Carmel, CA
1984 – Davis Duplex, 171 San Carlos Avenue, Sausalito, CA
1984 – Belinda and Jim Holliday Residence, Carmel, CA
1984 – Ernest Reddick Residence, 138 Hillside Avenue, Piedmont, CA
1985 – Robert Taylor Residence, Sausalito, CA
1985 – Boris Lakusta Residence, 120 Locust Avenue, San Rafael, CA
1985 – Libby and Bill Clark Residence, Carmel Highlands, CA
1986 – Davis Construction Shack, Inverness, CA
1987 – Willard Clark Residence, 15840 10th Avenue, Hanford, CA
1987 – RW Moore Residence, Windcrest Road, Rye, NY
1988 – Mueller Dovecote and Garage
1988 – Jim & Fa Lu Hutson Residence, Grizzly Peak State
1989 – Tyler and Jane Mann Residence, Inverness, CA
1989 – Joseph Phelps Vineyards Garden, St. Helena, CA
1989 – Joseph Phelps Vineyards Winery Addition, St. Helena, CA
1989 – Casey Residence, 943 Sea Eagle Loop, Bodega Bay, CA
1990 – Zeiser Residence, Lake Delavan
1991 – Gill Residence, San Anselmo, CA
1991 – Karen Barbour Residence, 30 Drakes View Drive, Inverness, CA
1992 – Murray and Mariette Trelease Residence, 343 Eagles Roost Lane,
           Lopez Island, WA
1992 – Alexander Julian Residence, 323 Florida Hill Road, Ridgefield, CT

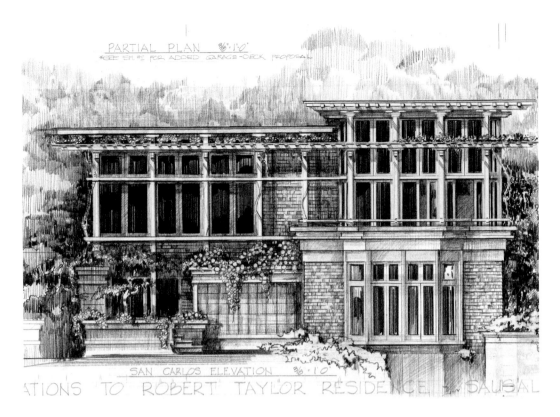

Taylor Residence, Sausalito, CA. 1985.

1993 – Shoaf Residence, Wichita, KS
1993 – Dr. and Mrs. Philip Mann Residence, Taylor Road, Tiburon, CA
1993 – Garland Wood Residence, American Virgin Islands
1994 – JM Davis Residence, Lopez Island, WA
1994 – John Thacher Remodel, 1663 Scott Street, St. Helena, CA
1995 – Keeney Residence, Russellville, AR
1995 – Dr. & Mrs. Philip Mann Residence, 325 Taylor Road, Tiburon, CA
1996 – Robert & Norma Wells Residence, 366 Via del Vista, Inverness, CA
1997 – Davis Residence, 430 Aberdeen Way, Inverness, CA
1997 – Jim Trees Residence, 2582 Filbert Street, San Francisco, CA
1997 – Durrie Garden
1997 – GG & Larry Green Landscape, 18 Mirabel Avenue, Mill Valley, CA
1998 – Bransten Landscape, 2775 Filbert Street, San Francisco, CA
1998 – Shoaf Residence, Aspen, CO
1999 – Joseph Phelps Vineyards Smokehouse, St. Helena, CA
1999 – Jim and Katherine Lino Residence, 55 Laurel Street, Inverness, CA
2001 – Ho Shin & Katy Davis Song Guest House, 34 Meadow Street, Mill Valley, CA
2003 – Marty & Katie Rapozo Landscape, 17244 High Road, Sonoma, CA
2003 – Gray Residence, Berkeley, CA
2005 – Mary O'Donouvan Residence, 2131 Vistazo E. Street, Tiburon, CA

UNDATED PROJECTS

Michael and Diane Wakelin Residence, Mill Valley, CA
Setrakian Residence, 266 Seadrift Road, Stinson Beach, CA
Smith Residence, Wichita, KS
Residence, 1745 Bridgeway, Sausalito, CA
Dirk Van Waart, Kitchen
Kramlich Residence, Oakville, CA
McMahon Project, Flagstaff, Az
Drake Project, Stinson Beach, CA
Bill Jones Residence, Greenbrae, CA
Jim & Rosemary Peterson Residence, Piedmont, CA
Schaal Residence, Portola Valley, CA
Davis Residence, 10 Arenal Avenue, Stinson Beach, CA
De Ruff Landscape, 3 Southwood Avenue, Ross, CA
David and Marilyn Baum, Landscape, 561 Summit Avenue, Mill Valley, CA
Robert Evans Residence, Stinson Beach, CA
Dr. Mark and Elizabeth Levy Residence, Cloverdale, CA
Claire Arnold Guest House, Lopez Island, WA

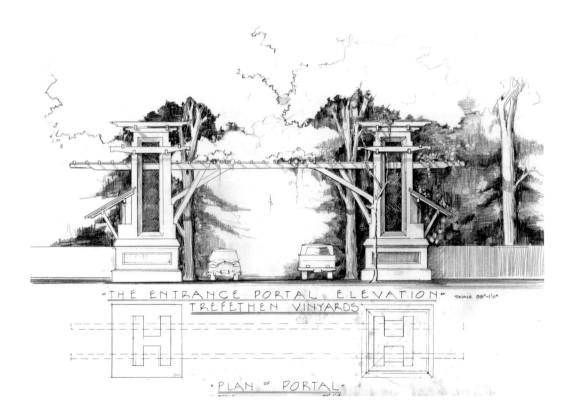

Trefethen Vineyards, Napa CA.

Mann Residence, Tiburon, CA. 1993.

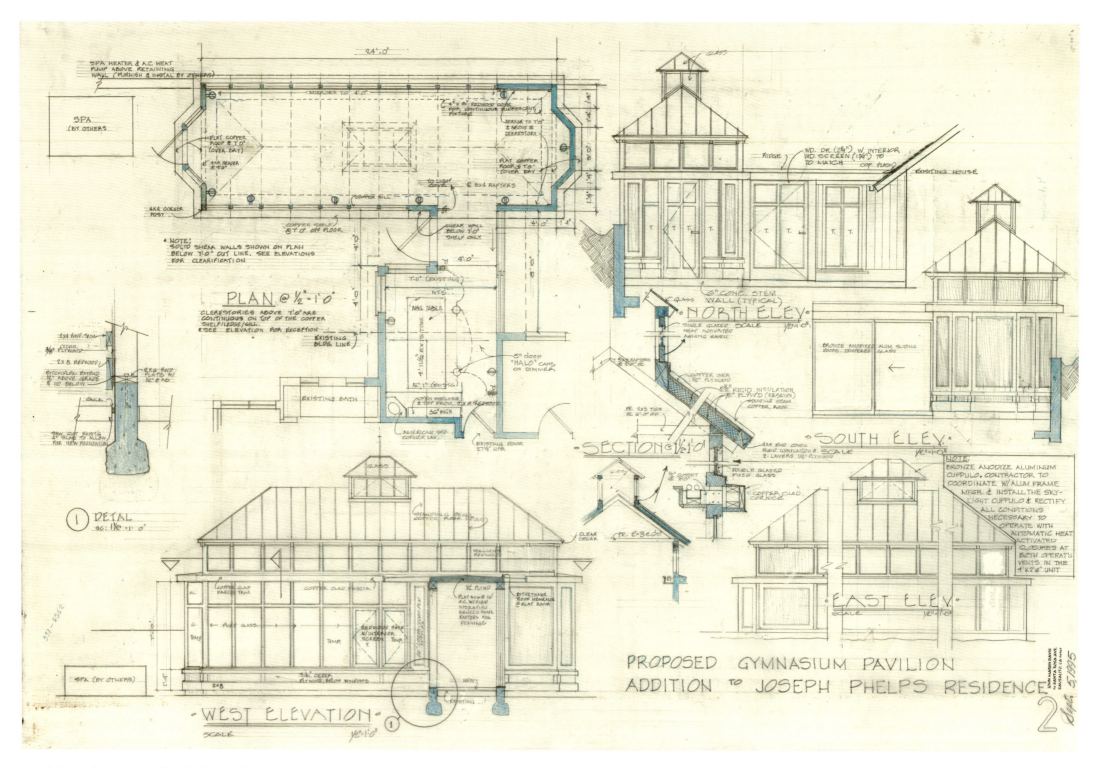

Joseph Phelps Gymnasium addition. St. Helena, CA | 1995.

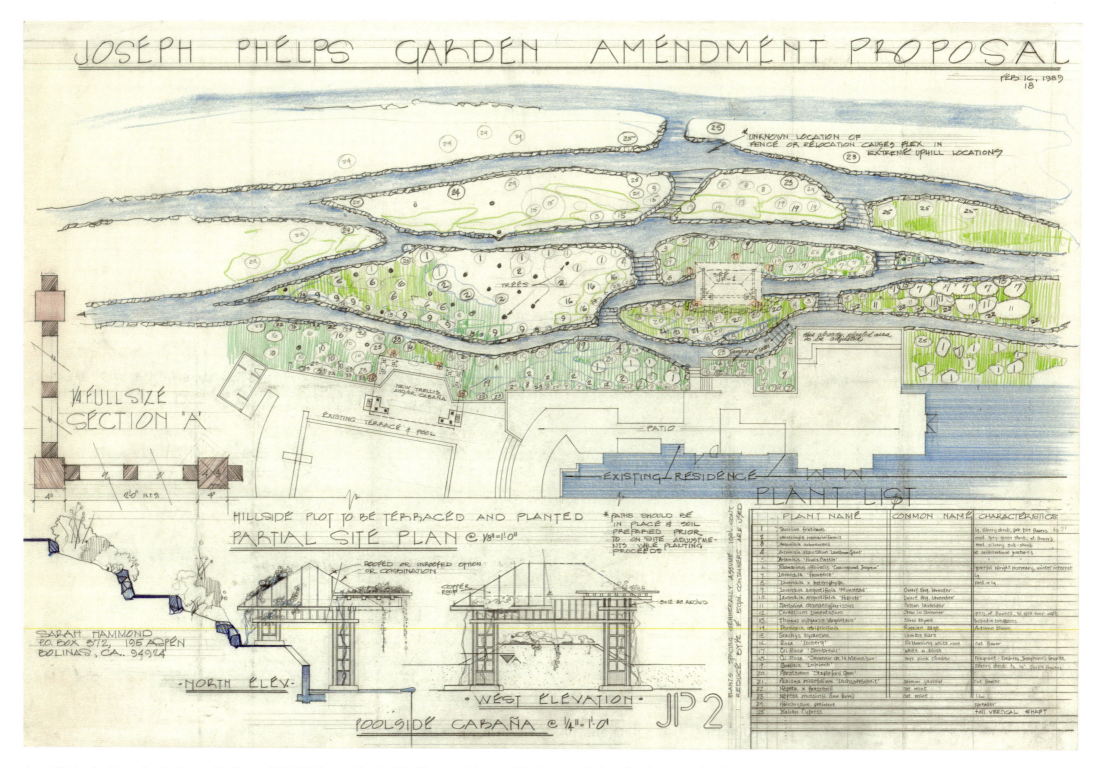

Joseph Phelps Residence Garden Proposal St. Helena, CA | 1989. As noted by David Sheff's essay, John turned his attention to his love of landscapes and gardens.

INDEX

PHOTOGRAPHY AND IMAGE SOURCES

Primary photography by Bruce Damonte and R. Brad Knipstein Photography. Family album images and architectural drawings courtesy of the John Marsh Davis Family unless otherwise noted.

Bruce Damonte Cover, 009-010, 034, 053, 056, 062, 064, 066-067, 069, 107, 112-115, 118-119, 150-151, 154-155, 168-169, 174-175, 178-189, 191, 197, 199-200, 225, 228-233.
R. Brad Knipstein 006, 034, 083-084, 088-103, 203, 208-219.
Public Domain 016, 028, 032.
Oklahoma Publishing Company Photography Collection, OHS 028.
L.S. Slevin - Calisphere, "Photograph of Bernard Maybeck, Architect". Created: 25 November 1919 028.
Marion Brenner 021, 024.
Roberto Soncin Gerometta 022-023.
Robert A. Bowlby Architectural Slides, Box 1, Folder 1. American School of Architecture Archive, Western History Collections, University of Oklahoma Libraries 031.
Mark Millstein of Golden Gate Sotheby's International Realty 1035, 39, 142-149.
Courtesy of Donald MacDonald Architects 036.
Photo courtesy of Michele Muennig (daugher) 036.
G.K. "Mickey" Muennig Architectural Papers and Drawings, Box 56, Folder 5. American School of Architecture Archive, Western History Collections, University of Oklahoma Libraries. 036
Violeta Autumn Architectural Drawings and Photographs, American School of Architecture Archive, Western History Collections, University of Oklahoma Libraries 036.
Warren Callister Collection, Environmental Design Archives, UC Berkeley 038.
First Unitarian Church of San Francisco, Warren Callister Collection, Environmental Design Archives, UC Berkeley 038.
Hans R. Baldauf 038.
Margot Hartford 042, 049, 051.
California Home Magazine, Scans courtesy of Nancy Barbour 046-048, 050.
© Jason Wells Photography and Golden Gate Creative reserve all rights to all images shot 121, 124-125, 127.
© Tim Bies 129, 135-136.
David Diffenderfer 156.
Courtesy of Joseph Phelps Vineyards 173.
Dennis O'Kelly 196, 198.
Jak Wonderly 196, 201.
House Beautiful Magazine (1984) 221-223.

BOOK CREDITS

Coordination and research by Julia Stenderup, Peter Sterling and Hana Meihan Davis
Preliminary layout by Robert Holloway
Graphic design by Florencia Damilano
Art direction by Oscar Riera Ojeda
Copy editing by Kit Maude & Michael W. Phillips Jr.

OSCAR RIERA OJEDA
PUBLISHERS

Text and images copyright © 2022 Hans Baldauf, BCV Architecture + Interiors
Copyright © 2022 Hans Baldauf, BCV Architecture + Interiors and Oscar Riera Ojeda Publishers Limited
Text for "A Midwestern Renegade comes to California" copyright © 2022 David Sheff
Book design copyright © 2022 BCV Architecture + Interiors and Oscar Riera Ojeda Publishers Limited
ISBN 978-1-946226-67-9
Published by Oscar Riera Ojeda Publishers Limited
Printed in China

Oscar Riera Ojeda Publishers Limited
Unit 1331, Beverley Commercial Centre,
87-105 Chatham Road South, Tsim Sha Tsui, Kowloon, Hong Kong

Production Offices
Suit 19, Shenyun Road,
Nanshan District, Shenzhen 518055, China

International Customer Service & Editorial Questions: +1-484-502-5400

www.oropublishers.com | www.oscarrieraojeda.com
oscar@oscarrieraojeda.com

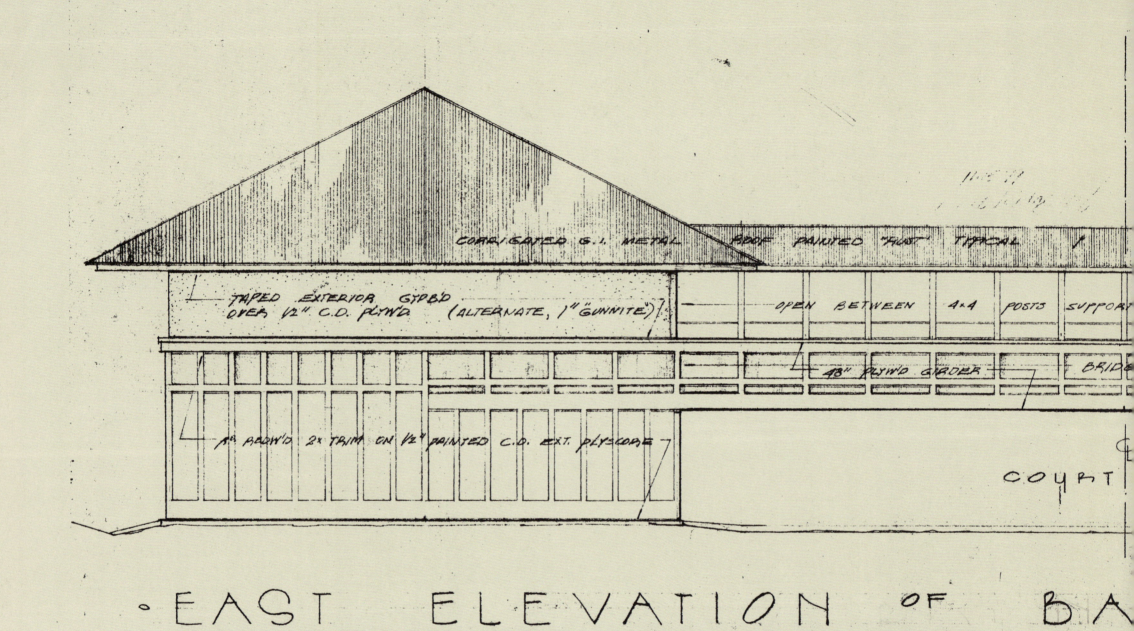

CORRUGATED G.I. METAL ROOF PAINTED "RUST" TYPICAL

TAPED EXTERIOR GYP.BD
OVER 1/2" C.D. PLYWD (ALTERNATE, 1" GUNNITE)

OPEN BETWEEN 4x4 POSTS SUPPORT

48" PLYWD GIRDER BRIDE

A" REQ'D 2x TRIM ON 1/2" PAINTED C.D. EXT. PLYSCORE

COURT

EAST ELEVATION OF BA

SCALE